The Problem of the Passions

THE PROBLEM OF THE PASSIONS

Feminism, Psychoanalysis, and Social Theory

Cynthia Burack

New York University Press
NEW YORK AND LONDON

New York University Press
New York and London

Library of Congress Cataloging-in-Publication Data
Burack, Cynthia, 1958–
The problem of the passions : feminism, paychoanalysis, and social
theory / Cynthia Burack.
p.   cm.
Includes bibliographical references (p.   ) and index.
ISBN 0-8147-1208-8
1. Feminist theory.   2. Emotions.   3. Psychoanalysis.   4. Object
relations (Psychoanalysis)   I. Title.
HQ1190.B85   1994   93-22153
305.42—dc20   CIP

New York University Press books are printed on acid-free paper, and their binding
materials are chosen for strength and durability.

Manufactured in the United States of America

10   9   8   7   6   5   4   3   2   1

To the memory of Virginia Olyn Sumpter

Contents

Acknowledgments

For their inspiration and for their careful and thoughtful readings of this manuscript, I would like to thank Fred Alford, Jim Glass, Ron Terchek, and Evelyn Beck. For additional suggestions on parts of the manuscript I am grateful to Jyl Josephson, Jeff Mann, and Phyllis Palmer. Tara Spigai, Susan Berger, and Alayna Waldrum provided patient and efficient research assistance. Friends, too numerous to mention, have been by turns supportive, critical, and outrageous through the years. Thank you all for making my work agreeable.

Excerpts from chapter 2, entitled "A House Divided: /Feminism and Object Relations Theory," appeared in *Women's Studies International Forum*, 15(4), 1992, 499–506. Excerpts from chapter 4, entitled "Love, Rage, and Destruction: Donald Winnicott and Social Theory," appeared in *Psychoanalysis and Contemporary Thought*, 16(3), 1993.

Finally, I wish to thank the Wallace Literary Agency, Inc., and Alfred A. Knopf, Inc., for granting me permission to quote from *The Moon Is Always Female* by Marge Piercy. Copyright © 1980 by Marge Piercy; Farrar, Straus and Giroux, Inc., and Faber and Faber, Ltd., for an excerpt from *For Your Own Good* by Alice Miller, translated by Hildegarde and Hunter Hannum. Translation copyright © 1983 by Alice Miller; Harper Collins Publishers for an excerpt from *Their Eyes Were Watching God* by Zora Neale Hurston, copyright renewed 1965 by John C. Hurston and Joel Hurston. Foreword copyright 1990 by Mary Helen

Washington. Afterword, Selected Bibliography, and Chronology copyright by Henry Louis Gates, Jr.; Allen & Unwin for an excerpt from "The 'anti-feminism' of Hannah Arendt" in *Hannah Arendt: Thinking, Judging, Freedom,* edited by Gisela T. Kaplan and Clive S. Kessler. Copyright © 1989 by G. T. Kaplan and C. S. Kessler.

The Problem of the Passions

Introduction

A silence surrounds certain of the passions in everyday social life. Although we know from intimate experience the ubiquity of rage, hatred, and other negative passions, such passions are rarely accorded the attention and scrutiny given to more pleasant aspects of human experience. This is not surprising; it is disquieting to dwell on the negative, and especially on the negative within oneself. It is easier, and can appear more constructive, to grant reality only to the positive, even at the risk of disowning parts of the self.

Feminists are acquainted with passions of rage and hatred, realized in the course of struggling to know feelings that have been denied. At the same time feminists are also forced to recognize the rage, fear, and hatred of others whose stable self- and social understandings are challenged by feminist beliefs and acts. In spite of (and perhaps because of) such experience, feminists are no less prone than many others to imagine and work toward an ideal world of relations from which these distressing and dispiriting passions have been excised.

Social and political theorists have long wrestled with the passions as a political conundrum. The passions have been understood as constructing certain forms of knowledge and community, and as rupturing others. Yet theorists have also been ambivalent about the passions. They have been particularly ambivalent about women's passions, and it is possible that this tension is motivated by the suspicion that attending to the passions and their role in social life illuminates much of what is active and creative—and therefore anarchic and disruptive—about the self.

Feminists have long challenged normative accounts of selfhood and subjectivity that disempower women's feelings, thought, speech, and action. In the modern Western philosophic tradition, selfhood has frequently been depicted as solitary, rational, principled, abstract, and genderless. Feminist theorists implicate such an account of selfhood in the perpetuation of women's oppression and systematically deny its adequacy to describe the multiplicity of women's historic experiences and values.

By reconceptualizing accounts of passion—including the role of the passions in constituting human beings as moral and political actors—feminists have often related differently to the passions than have other thinkers, adopting a unique, dual strategy in thinking about them. The first move is to demonstrate the feminine capacity for nurturance, love, empathy, and care for others; the second is to rescue the capacity of the self so reconstructed in terms of moral and political agency—that which has been denied to emotional beings in general, or women in particular.

With few exceptions, accounts of human nature in Western enlightenment political thought are embedded in, and inextricable from, assumptions about human nature, or the nature of self, that exclude women. These accounts have been, and continue to be, buttressed by arguments and assumptions about the "public" sphere as male and the "private" as female. In addressing the role of passion in the constitution of selves and communities, feminist theorists have critiqued much of the modern Western political tradition.

Prior to the twentieth century, feminists had already begun to challenge this dichotomy of "public" and "private" spheres and the content ascribed to them in theory and practice. Yet the resuscitation of the place of passions has been a more recent development in feminism. It has been encouraged by increasing interest in and use of the diverse psychologies, and especially by the wedding of feminism with psychoanalysis. However, most feminist theory continues to focus on the emotions that have been understood either as part of women's nature, or as necessary to women's caretaking functions. The ostensibly less functional, less "natural," passions in women have suffered philosophic neglect.

Moral and political philosopher David Hume called passions such as anger, rage, and hatred "disagreeable."[1] Hume recognized and theorized the salience of passion in moral selfhood in a way that is unmatched by other early-modern Western political thinkers. Although such praise is probably exaggerated, Hume's attention to the role of emotions in moral life might arguably earn him recognition as "the women's moral theorist."[2] It is nonetheless true that Hume's language regarding the passions suggests no disapprobation and invites no value judgment on the experience of these passions.

There is no [wo]man who, on particular occasions, is not affected with all the disagreeable passions, fear, anger, dejection, grief, melancholy, anxiety, etc. But these, so far as they are natural and universal, make no difference between one [wo]man and another, and can never be the object of blame.[3]

The disagreeable passions are not absent in women; indeed, they have empowered the "second wave" of feminism. Feminists have spoken of the need to mobilize passions denied to women in the service of political action, social change, and consciousness raising. In spite of this, and amid the fervor of discovering and employing depths of rage, despair, and hatred, an analytic gap has emerged within feminist theory. To say that feminist theory has failed adequately to theorize their existence would be to indict a literature that is now too vast to summarize responsibly. However, one variety of feminist theory has been in a unique position to provide a basis for understanding the disagreeable passions, yet has been unable consistently to do so.

A particularly important body of feminist theory has often failed, in investigating the roots of gender identity, community, and power, to theorize the place of these passions, especially in women. This is a consequential omission. The avoidance or marginalization of disagreeable passions stymies feminist theory in its attempt to construct an alternative to popular or tenacious representations of reality in social and political thought. Feminist theory can respond to these, but it is first necessary to reconstruct such theories to accommodate what has been left unspoken.

In the following chapters feminist versions of psychoanalytic object relations theory (Nancy Chodorow, Jessica Benjamin, and Dorothy Dinnerstein) and the work of academic psychologist Carol Gilligan are analyzed. Together, the work of these four theorists constitutes a body of feminist psychological social (or "psycho-social") theory, a characterization that testifies to the interdisciplinary and integrative nature of the work.

These theories are especially well suited to exploring the place of the passions. They probe the ontology of forms of human connection that have been consistently unrecognized in or banished from the public sphere and made invisible in political theory. They analyze the defensive nature and functions of that rationality so esteemed in modern Western politics and philosophy. Moreover, they identify and challenge the gendered nature and attribution of diverse forms of connection. In particular, the work of object relations feminists analyzes the nature of social relations at the same time that it interrogates the deep psychological structure of gender identity.[4]

Feminists have appropriated and modified aspects of the psychoanalytic object relations tradition. In some cases they have created unique systems of thought from foundations in this tradition. At the same time, they have borrowed selectively from object relations theory, and thereby left behind much that might be useful for conceptualizing passions such as rage and hatred. Thus, this book illustrates how feminist theory might benefit from taking seriously excluded aspects of the object relations tradition, and especially the insights of a pioneer of object relations theory, Melanie Klein.

It is difficult to characterize collectively the ideas that are understood here to constitute feminist psycho-social theory. At its best, feminist psycho-social theory attempts to discover the creative processes at the core of the self's confrontation with the world. Especially as they are posited in object relations theory, these processes are neither entirely of the self nor of the outside world; instead, they are both.

One way of conceiving of object relations theory, elaborated in chapter 2, is as a body of ideas that is oriented to discovering and explaining the mechanisms by which the passions and all of mental life develop, increase in complexity, and produce outcomes for the self and for others in society. Feminists who have used object relations theory have understood well that it endows the self with agency while retaining the dissonances, paradoxes, and latent meanings of emotions. The problem in feminist psychological social theory is not that it has failed to apprehend the significance of the passions; in fact, the recognition of them has been one of its greatest strengths.

The problem is that ambivalence toward the disagreeable passions, and what Melanie Klein and others believe to be an understandable desire in humans to deceive ourselves about their ubiquity, is inscribed in much feminist theory. An ambivalent or avoident stance toward passions of rage and hatred in feminist theory is not complete; some theories integrate these passions better than others. Many arguments, however, do not conceptualize rage, hatred, and aggression with the vigor expended on more positive passions. And when these disagreeable passions are made central to theory, they are often explained away as unfortunate products of problematic relations.

This weakness in feminist psycho-social thought must be redressed. It is especially critical to do so because feminist theory provides the means of analyzing, criticizing, and mending more "mainstream" accounts of the self, relations, and community in social and political thought. Psychologies of women have been incomparably useful to feminists in pointing out the psychologically vacuous assumptions about human beings that undergird political theories. Indeed, theorists of all descriptions are and will continue to be indebted to feminism for these interdisciplinary contributions. It is necessary now, however, to give greater attention to this work that has so enhanced our understanding of the deficiencies of traditional social and political theory; we must inquire into the assumptions of feminist psycho-social theories themselves as a next step in feminist critique.

One important mainstream account of the self-in-relation that has been the focus of feminist attention is derived from communitarian political theory. In its critique of the liberal account of the self, communitarian thought comes closest to exemplifying the concerns with community and the relational capacities of people characteristic of feminist theories. However, feminists are increasingly critical of communitarianism. Chapter 1 shows the reasons for this discomfort, and demonstrates the need for a more psychologically complex vision, one that can be supplied by an expanded feminism.

In chapter 2 the appropriation of object relations theory by feminists is examined in detail, and the argument is made that object relations theory has given feminists a paradigm for creating more viable theories of selfhood and relations than either liberalism or communitarianism. The inattention to the work of Melanie Klein on the part of feminists who borrow from object relations is problematic, however. The absence of Klein from feminist renderings of object relations accompanies a lack of interest in confronting disagreeable passions. As a theorist Klein represents and exemplifies these passions.

The most widely known of the feminist psychological accounts of the self, and one that does not employ object relations theory, is that of Carol Gilligan. Chapter 3 consists of an analysis of Gilligan's account of the female self. The argument of this chapter is that Gilligan's theory is damaged by her inattention to disagreeable passions and, further, that Gilligan's rejection of psychoanalysis is itself questionable. Gilligan's work provides a way of correcting some of the most egregious assumptions associated with the communitarian self, but does not go deeply enough to provide feminist theory with an alternative.

Such an alternative can emerge from a feminist object relations theory. First, however, it is essential to understand existing feminist applications of object relations, their flaws as well as their strengths. Chapter 4 analyzes two of the most prominent feminist object relations theories of women's identity, those of Nancy Chodorow and Jessica Benjamin. Both Chodorow and Benjamin are successful in having conceptualized the self as gendered, and as impassioned. Even so, their insights falter when they confront the more troublesome aspects of identity, and both flee to more optimistic uses of object relations theory, especially in the person of analyst-theorist Donald Winnicott.

Chapter 5 consists of a reconsideration of the appropriation of object relations theory by feminists, including the feminist propensity to substitute a tame and palliative vision of the self, represented by Winnicott, for a harsh and recalcitrant vision of the self, represented by Klein. The work of Dorothy Dinnerstein is presented as an example of theory that incorporates the ideas of Klein while, not surprisingly, taking seriously the disagreeable passions. Proceeding in this way would make available to social theory a reinvigorated version of object relations theory, one that feminists have initiated and that has the potential to provide a more sturdy foundation to social thought than the relational self of communitarianism.

CHAPTER I

The Passions and Theories of Community

Although the disclosure of who we are always demands the presence of others, it is possible not only in the public sphere "out there," but also, in different ways, in our most intimate relationships.

> —Maria Markus,
> "The 'anti-feminism' of Hannah Arendt"

The Self in Visions of Community

Nonfeminist political theorists often have not been explicit about the kind of "selves" that populate the polis as they envision it. Many integrate into their work in a piecemeal fashion particular key aspects of selfhood as required by their own projects. Human actors are endowed by theorists with characteristics, predispositions, motives, and attributes for the purpose of specific arguments about social and political life. These do not always constitute total and consistent visions; indeed, political theorists often prefer to remain agnostic about such questions, or to insist that their political and philosophic ideas do not presuppose any particular answer to them.

Feminist theorists have been less reluctant as a group to debate and theorize about the nature of the self. This is in large part because feminists find political and social theories to be rife with descriptions of, and assumptions about, human beings in which women are not represented. Such locutions as *man* and *men* do not only fail to satisfy some abstract standard of equal linguistic treatment; rather, they mystify the meaning of theoretical discourse and the exclusion of women from it. Even the use of more "generic" terms—*persons, citizens,* and the like—constitutes a kind of semantic shift that easily disguises the different experiences, desires, rights, roles, statuses, and legitimated aspirations of the sexes.

Feminists have thus found it necessary to critique the silence about women and sexual difference in social and political thought. To do so they have often turned to psychology. Crossing traditional disciplinary boundaries enables feminists to construct more subtle and complex accounts of the self. In these theories the self (sometimes more explicitly, the female self) is constituted through connection; a principle source, as well as consequence, of connection is emotionality, especially those emotions related to love, empathy, compassion, and nurturance. This emphasis on intimacy and on the emotions has been deliberate, for it is a way of rectifying exclusion.

Each of the theorists to be considered in the chapters ahead adamantly maintains from her own theoretical perspective the need for attention to the self and emotions in social theory. But the status of emotions and passionate selfhood in feminist theory requires reexamination. So thorough is the identification of care with feelings, of love with affectivity, that more disagreeable passions are often ignored. This neglect exacts a cost in the explanatory and prescriptive potential of feminist social thought.

Psychoanalytic object relations provides one way (though not, certainly, the only way) to reintegrate the disagreeable passions into feminist social theory. As a theoretical tool for such an enterprise it is particularly appropriate because it is already employed, albeit selectively, by many. Feminists who use object relations theory envision the self as passionate, contradictory, ambivalent in its very nature. This perspective does not deny gender difference, any more than it constructs a particular theory of gender difference. Indeed, in understanding the evolution of self as anchored in processes, defenses, emotional patterns, and developmental dilemmas negotiated with others, object relations leaves open more possibilities for theories of gender than it forecloses.

Feminist social theory that is grounded in psychology has been instrumental to the genesis of modern feminist theory. This contribution would nonetheless be enhanced by more thorough attention to the disagreeable passions and their role in shaping relations and community.

Relation in Feminist Theories of Community

What is available in feminist critiques of, and alternative accounts of, selfhood is a self that is constituted in and through a network of delicate and difficult processes of connection.[1] In women, this affiliativeness is usually understood as cause, consequence, or both, of emotions like love or empathy. So, for example, Carol Gilligan, playing with the themes of "attachment" and "detachment," concludes that "attachments arise from the human capacity to move others and be moved by them."[2] Gilligan, as we shall see, specifies not incorrectly, but too narrowly, what is involved in moving others and being moved by them.

In the perspective described above is often embedded a tacit understanding that the disagreeable passions are the undoing of relations rather than kinds of relations. Yet rage and hatred are passions that presuppose a world of others. Not only this; they can also be constitutive of attachments, of relations with others. Male theorists have pursued this insight more diligently than have female theorists. Psychoanalyst Vamik Volkan stresses the bonding that mutual hatred can accomplish in his psychoanalytic study of international relations.[3] Similarly, Richard Sennett reminds in *Authority*[4] of the ways in which even painful, hateful, and dysfunctional authority relations can create virtually indissoluble forms of connection. As Murray Edelman puts it, "Enmity is a bond as well as a divider."[5]

By now many feminists have explored not only the new questions and opportunities, but also the problems created by feminist notions of affiliation and community. Mary Dietz argues that women's political action should not be identified with women's intimate care and mothering. Invoking Hannah Arendt, Dietz suggests that love cannot be "marshaled for political ends" except at the risk of having the "outside world taint or break" it.[6] Joan Tronto suggests that a morality of care provides more than opportunities and imperatives for nourishing relationships; it may also furnish the basis for "hatreds of difference" as people choose unreflectively to protect existing forms of relations.[7]

More contentious is Catharine MacKinnon's claim that the "different voice" of love and care established by Gilligan as the sine qua non of women's morality is in reality "the voice of the victim," feeling, and speaking, from a position of powerlessness.[8] Marcia Westkott criticizes some feminist psychologists not only for identifying the mother-daughter bond as uncritically positive, but also for presenting it as a model for desirable—empathic and nondestructive—social relations.[9] Vast differences clearly coexist within feminism about how to conceptualize, and then perhaps create, normative forms of connection and relatedness. Most feminists agree, however, that settled distinctions between "public" and "private" spheres of human activity are properly subjects of challenge and debate. Some form of this assumption can, in fact, be located in the work of feminist psycho-social theorists and their critics. Just such an assumption is evident in feminist attempts to theorize about the different varieties of human relations—the realization that these have implications for feminist psychological and social theory, and practice.

Feminists are not, however, the only contemporary social critics who understand the self as inextricable from its relations with others. The comparison of two accounts of the self, feminist and communitarian, demonstrates that central themes of feminist discourse about the self are also to be found in the works of other traditions of social and political thought. However, if feminist and communitarian theories are similar in many of their concerns, they also achieve quite different levels of success in addressing these concerns. This difference of success, in both the feminist and communitarian projects, can be understood in one important respect as a function of the account of the passions that issues from each.

The Communitarian Critics of Liberalism

Nonfeminist political theory has in recent years yielded a body of literature that has sought to expose the inadequacies of the variants of liberal theory. The theorists have come to be called collectively "communitarian critics of liberalism," in spite of an absence of any agreed-upon criteria for the inclusion of particular works or ideas into the communitarian "canon." Among the more influential of those placed in the category of communitarian theorists are: Bruce Ackerman, Michael Sandel, Alasdair MacIntyre, Benjamin Barber, Philip Green, Richard Rorty, and Roberto

Unger; but this list is far from being exhaustive. Conceding that it is difficult to identify "representative" communitarians, the discussion that follows will concentrate on works of Sandel and MacIntyre.

The inadequacies of liberal theories are understood by recent communitarian critics to be especially evident in the failure of liberal theory to construct and defend persuasive accounts: first, of the self (that are not, in the words of Amy Gutman, "irreparably individualistic") and, second, of stronger forms of community than appear possible, or desirable, to liberals. Communitarian writings have in turn inspired an increasing number of feminist responses, which appear to grow more critical of communitarian ideas. The feminist reaction to communitarian philosophy is revealing; examining it permits the development of a critical perspective not only on communitarian theory itself (which would have been possible in some form without the feminist critique), but also on some mutual aims and interests of communitarian and feminist thought.

What perspectives on the nature of self do communitarian theory and feminist theory share? How do feminist political theorists conceptualize the failures of the communitarian project? In what ways do feminist psycho-social theories carry out the communitarian project of constructing a more adequate account of the self more effectively than communitarians themselves? How does the integration of the disagreeable passions into feminist theory abet the feminist execution of a "communitarian" project? I shall argue that feminist psycho-social theories, modified to respond to and integrate the disagreeable passions, provide a more adequate foundation for an account of the self in community than those of communitarian theory.

The Self in Communitarian Philosophy

In characterizing the debate between communitarians and liberals, Gutman points out that contemporary communitarians are unlike some earlier critics in that they emerge from an Aristotelian, rather than a Marxian, tradition. Whatever else might be said of this difference in origins and its ramifications, philosophers in the "Aristotelian" tradition have frequently sought to theorize about the nature of the good citizen, "man," or polis. Aristotle himself gives serious attention to the nature of passions and their relation to a "good" life. On the subject of anger he says, among other things:

It is human to be painfully affected by anger.[10]

Anger may be produced by a variety of causes, but, however that may be, it is the man who is angry on the right occasions and with the right people and at the right moment who wins our commendation.[11]

The trouble about anger would seem to be that, while it does to some extent listen to reason, it does not hear it aright.[12]

For Machiavelli, the political world is infused with passions of all descriptions. Some of these, on the parts of rulers or the ruled, constitute impediments to the survival of the state, whereas others may be indulged to salutary effect. However he confronts them, Machiavelli does not abstract the passions out of social life. Anger, envy, hatred are inherent in human nature; the sovereign, and citizens, ignore them at their peril. Perhaps it is proper to understand contemporary communitarians as rooted, as Gutman suggests, in an Aristotelian tradition. If this is so, it is appropriate to suggest at the outset that contemporary communitarian thought abandons at least a part of what is perspicacious in the work of predecessors.

Communitarians have distinguished their own accounts of the self from those produced within liberal theories.[13] They have conceptualized liberal accounts of the self in a number of ways: as empirically inadequate, as subversive of certain kinds of communities and self-reflections, and as, on the whole, ideological constructs posing as value-free description. In his essay "The Communitarian Critique of Liberalism," Michael Walzer sets out a critical perspective on the communitarian account of the self. Simply put, he suggests that the communitarian critique is confused—that communitarians make two disparate claims. The first is that liberal theory has contributed to the construction of persons in liberal societies who really are "liberal selves" (deracinated, dissociated, acquisitive, self-interested). The second is that liberal theory misunderstands the nature of persons; real selves are more nearly communitarian than they are "liberal selves."

This is a lucid delineation of arguments that at times elide within the same theory. It makes possible further clarifications. In terms of the first kind of criticism, communitarian theorists often presuppose that the self is a faithful reflection of the community, of whatever sort that community (or its ideology) might be. Hence, Walzer notes that in attacking liberal societies as having resulted in the formation of liberal selves, "liberal theory now seems to have a power over and against real life that has been granted to few theories in human history."[14] According to this view, liberalism has made the persons within its purview as surely as would stronger, more historically rooted forms of communal life make other, different persons.

The second kind of criticism located by Walzer indicates that communitarians also insist upon a subterranean interpenetration of self and community that may not be recognized or legitimated by theory or ideology. Thus, in the real world persons are bound to others in relations of mutuality and historical understanding that help to constitute them as certain kinds of persons. And this in spite of the absence of fertile ground in liberal societies for such deep and defining forms of attachment.

Given this confusion, how can the communitarian account of the self be represented? Walzer conceptualizes the debate between communitarians and liberals in this way: "The central issue for political theory is not the constitution of the self but the connection of constituted selves, the pattern of social relations."[15] Feminist psycho-social theorists would not disagree so much as merely add that these are inextricable issues. Walzer finds interest in, and concern with, "the connection of constituted selves" within the deep structure of liberal theory. Nonetheless, it is undeniable that such interest and concern is a less ambivalent (and more explicit) theme of feminist and communitarian theory. But Walzer's insight is interesting because it is consistent with the perspective from which both the present critique and the accounts of feminist psycho-social theorists come: To examine the self is to examine the self in its relations with others. To examine the self in its relations with others, theorists must recognize the passions. One commentator argues that communitarians do just this.

Evan Simpson characterizes the project of communitarians (whom he calls "moral conservatives") as grounding political morality in "human relationships." His reading of the communitarian response to the rationalism of the liberals is that to them, "the permanent aspect of human existence is the reality of ordinary attachments and conflicts."[16] From this interest in historically and socially particular relations Simpson derives a communitarian concern with the passions "fear, curiosity, hope, pity" as well as "pride, love . . . anger." It is reasonable for communitarian philosophers to concern themselves with the passions, he argues, for "human psychology is more convincing as a basis for morality than are undemonstrable metaphysical notions of 'common humanity.' "[17]

At least in this respect, Simpson extrapolates from his own interpretation of communitarian philosophy. This is true in two ways. First, tracing the communitarian account of the self from a concern with social relations to a recognition of the pertinence of human psychology appears sensible, yet it is by no means obvious that this is the path taken by communitarians. It is difficult, in fact, to find evidence that communitarians attempt to embed their account of the self in any coherent psychology. Second, analyses of the passions and their role in helping to constitute the self are scarce in the majority of communitarian texts.[18] These claims cannot be conclusively demonstrated in a brief survey of communitarian works. Such a survey can, however, suggest the tenor of communitarian accounts of the self.

Two Communitarian Accounts of the Self

Michael Sandel's *Liberalism and the Limits of Justice* is most obviously a critique of John Rawls's influential *Theory of Justice*. The subtext of this critique, a more sweeping indictment of liberal theory, cannot, however, be ignored. For it is in the context of this more inclusive critique that Sandel's contribution to a communitarian account of the self may be found.

Sandel characterizes the subject of liberal theory as an "antecedently individuated self."[19] This characterization is grounded in two assumptions that Sandel exhumes from liberal thought. The first is an assumption of "mutual disinterest" among persons, or the notion that "we are distinct individuals first and then (circumstances permitting) we form relationships and engage in cooperative arrangements with others."[20] The second, related, assumption according to Sandel is that identity is independent of a person's ends, values, interests, and relations with others; this is the notion that these can never be understood as constitutive of who one is, but only as freely chosen.

Counterposed to this "antecedently individuated self" is Sandel's own "constitutive conception of the self." The distinction between these perspectives lies principally in the fact that according to the constitutive view, identity is "defined to some extent by the community."[21] The key phrase in this definition may be Sandel's qualification, "to some extent," for it is unclear what is signified by it. Marilyn Friedman's intuition is that communitarians suggest a more totalizing vision of the self as a reflection of its community,[22] an insight that is consistent with Walzer's wry comment on the power imputed to liberal theory by communitarians.

Sandel is aware of the dilemma; he maintains that neither conception, of a rigidly antecedent self or a self "engulf[ed]" by its environment, is desirable. But the solution that he proposes, a self that can through reflection "participate in the constitution of its identity," is not as successful as he presumes.[23] The suggestion that the self is at every moment able to "turn its lights inward upon itself" in such a way as to evaluate strongly the nature of its relation to its own desires is insufficient in two respects.

First, the independence of the self from the community referenced by this strategy of reflection is not much in evidence throughout Sandel's argument. This is particularly easy to understand because much of Sandel's argument is an attempt to distance his own views from a model of presocial liberal individualism. More interesting, however, is a second kind of failure. Even if reflection is the self's means of denying the hegemony of the community and contributing to its own constitution, reflection alone cannot fully illuminate and dispense with the stubborn and conflictual nature of the passions.[24] And this is so although the claim for evaluation is that it reaches to the possibility of reflecting upon and reconsidering the "object[s] of desire."

Charles Taylor concedes that even self-reflection and evaluation have limits. The "deepest evaluations" of who one is as a self "are least clear, least articulated, most easily subject to illusion and distortion." What is the result for reflection, or evaluation of the self? "It is those [evaluations] which are closest to what I am as a subject, in the sense that shorn of them I would break down as a person, which are among the hardest for me to be clear about."[25] In other words, the theory of self-evaluation upon which Sandel depends to articulate the personal and anarchic dimension of the self to its community is likely not to reach to those deepest aspects of selfhood. Sandel does not perceive this as a problem in his rendering of the nature of the self because he does not appear to tie the formation of the self in its relations to a world of others as necessitating passions of love and hate. Sandel is left advancing both of the communitarian arguments delineated by Walzer. On the one hand, he suggests that the self is a reflection of its community, whereas on the other, he asserts the essentially social nature of the self, although in the absence of any serious consideration of the passions.

Alasdair MacIntyre's enterprise in *After Virtue* is ostensibly quite different from that of Sandel in *Liberalism and the Limits of Justice*. Whereas Sandel dissects a particular version of liberal theory, MacIntyre seeks to defend a modified Aristotelian account of the virtues against the "enlightenment project" of morality. His indictments are thus of modernity, and not just liberalism, although in deconstructing modernity, liberal moral thought is exposed as incoherent and dangerously inadequate. In the course of giving an account of the virtues, MacIntyre gives a compatible account of the self.

There is much more complexity to MacIntyre's account of the self than is captured in one of his more familiar passages:

It is not just that different individuals live in different social circumstances; it is also that we all approach our own circumstances as bearers of a particular social identity. I am someone's son or daughter, someone else's cousin or uncle; I am a citizen of this or that city, a member of this or that guild or profession; I belong to this clan, that tribe, this nation. Hence what is good for me has to be the good for one who inhabits these roles.[26]

It is difficult to imagine a vision of the relation of self to world that creates a more complete identity between them. Yet even in terms of MacIntyre's own ideas, this statement seems extreme. MacIntyre does, more than Sandel, write of the various roles conferred on the passions in moral theories, especially in analyzing Jane Austen's attention to them from her position as the last great representative of a "classical tradition of the virtues."[27] And he does argue that the mere fact of embeddedness in roles, communities, and historical eras does not bind the self so thoroughly as to leave no room for active remaking of the terms of existence.

Yet MacIntyre's error is that of most (moral and political) theorists. He anchors the self in its moral context only to ignore the significance for the constitution of the self of the vicissitudes of early life:

Despite his insistence that we think in terms of a complete human life—"a concept of a self whose unity resides in the unity of a narrative which links birth to life to death as narrative beginning to middle to end"—his moral subjects are apparently born directly into adulthood.[28]

Sandel is guilty of this omission as well. He imagines persons, possessed of "character" and "moral depth," at a level of abstraction that never suggests anything of, for example, the psychic and physical vulnerability of early life.

An objection might be that moral and political theorists are properly concerned with adults and adult relations. Why is the absence of any consideration of childhood relevant? As Judith Hughes points out in her witty look at children from the perspectives of philosophers, social thinkers have, throughout history, evinced interest in children. The most obvious reason for this interest "is the strong and well-founded belief that the experiences of childhood affect the kind of adult which the child turns out to be."[29] Further, typical accounts of the acquisition of reason by male children in the works of great philosophers leave unexplained "things like teaching and learning, or development in understanding and character and all those other concepts *which refer to processes and not to states.*"[30]

Hughes's argument is not psychoanalytic, but her insight lends itself easily to a psychoanalytic critique. Underlying much of the feminist object relations theory project are assumptions about the tenaciousness of continuities between early and later consciousness, the passions that attend them, and the social significance of these passions. Object relations theory conceptualizes these continuities predominantly in the form of processes. In such a formulation, the rigid discontinuity between irrational and rational, immature and mature, childhood and adulthood, dissolves; in its place is set a more fluid vision of development. The scope of the passions is exhausted neither by the investigation of roles nor by subjective self-assessments.

Susan Moller Okin does not raise this issue because of a concern with the deep nature of the self in communitarian theory. She pursues her point in order to highlight the irrelevance of certain kinds of moral subjects and virtues—namely women and the courage and strength required for socially necessary acts of childbirth and child rearing—to much moral theory. The criticism is, however, relevant to more psychological critiques of communitarian thought. To the extent that theorists like MacIntyre and Sandel overlook the ways in which the self from its beginnings comes into contact with the community, the characterization of liberal theories as the work of men who have forgotten their childhoods applies to communitarian theories as well.

The communitarian attempt to characterize and ground the self has not always been seen as problematic to feminists. Indeed, comparison between some central aspects of the work of communitarians and that of Carol Gilligan reveals similar conclusions. Lorraine Code, for instance, treats MacIntyre favorably, comparing him with Gilligan. She notes MacIntyre's particularistic emphasis when he speaks of the importance of understanding morality in the context of the narrative unity of each life. The self is, for Gilligan (and, Code suggests, for MacIntyre) the subject of its own story, embedded in interlocking sets of relations. The characterization of Gilligan as attending to "how it is that actual, historically situated, gendered epistemological and moral subjects know and respond to actual, complex experiences" is extended to MacIntyre as well.[31]

It can be said of both Gilligan and MacIntyre that an important aspect of their work is the attempt to rectify a pervasive universalizing tendency of much modern theory. For both, the ability to treat others justly and morally presupposes webs of relations in which persons are embedded, and not abstract claims to justice. MacIntyre, like Gilligan in some respects, attends also to the transformative potential of conflict, both within communities and within the self: "It is through conflict and sometimes only through conflict that we learn what our ends and purposes are."[32] As in much of Gilligan's theory, however, passions are simply not among the things—such as values, ends, obligations—whose conflicting nature can be understood as an intrinsic aspect of the contact between self and other.

MacIntyre ends, then, in much the same way as Sandel. The self is a reflection of the community, except in those ways in which conflicts between incommensurable obligations, values, and virtues make new and unforeseen resolutions possible. The passions remain beyond the scope of communitarian concern.

The Response of Feminist Political Theory

The nature of the feminist critique of communitarian philosophy is heavily influenced by its provenance; the critique has been carried out by feminist political philosophers, and not by those whose work is grounded in psychology. Two of the most penetrating analyses are made by Marilyn Friedman in her essay "Feminism and Modern Friendship: Dislocating the Community" and Susan Moller Okin in her book *Justice, Gender, and the Family.* These works are enormously useful guides to previously unexplored flaws in the communitarian vision, particularly in terms of the assumptions about, and implications for, women of that vision. What these critiques do not provide is available from other areas of feminist theory—more specifically, from feminist psycho-social theory. It is possible to supplement the extant feminist critique with one that is sensitive to a broader variety of issues, but first it is useful to see how feminists do engage communitarian ideas.

Friedman warns that communitarian thought is a "perilous ally" for feminism, and Okin appears to concur. What is the nature of this reticence regarding communitarianism? Between them, Okin and Friedman identify a number of problematic elements in communitarianism. For Okin the critical inadequacy of communitarian theory is its mystification of relations within the family and, hence, its tendency to ignore the need for the extension of principles of justice into the "private" life of the family. Her targets are the denied, unnoticed, and ostensibly "natural" forms of inequalities between the sexes that escape communitarian notice. She is concerned with demonstrating how the forms of community espoused by communitarians rest upon and presume women's nurturance, subservience, and/or exclusion.[33]

Friedman's critique begins by recognizing commonalities between the work of feminist theorists like Chodorow, Dinnerstein, and Gilligan and communitarian writers.[34] She then proceeds to outline what is problematic in communitarianism. The bulk of these criticisms are political in nature. One is that communitarians endorse, or remain unaware of, the tyrannical practices and moral claims of communities and the ways in which these affect both members and nonmembers. Some kinds of communities are, as Friedman claims, "characterized by practices of exclusion and suppression" that are essential, not incidental, to them.

Such a challenge affirms that communities are not neutral, ahistorical entities: communities constitute themselves and maintain their boundaries in a multitude of ways—through language, informal social practices, and more formal and routinized social institutions. Notions of membership (or inclusion) and outsider status (or exclusion) are consequences of constitutive strategies of communities that in turn help to shape and reinforce these same communities. Some persons belong, whereas others do not. But processes of constitution are even more subtle and complex: some persons belong by choice, whereas others are forcibly included; some choose not to belong, whereas others are forcibly ejected.

Another claim, made by both Friedman and Okin, is that historical communities have routinely relied upon the domination of some members by others—exemplary is the domination of women by men—in the framing and pursuit of their goals. Communities have routinely institutionalized domination of many sorts in the form of moral claims and appeals to nature, utility, and tradition. Once established, forms of domination, suppression, and exploitation can be remarkably resistant to exposure and reform. This the history of political thought amply demonstrates, and proponents of community fail to acknowledge.

The comments of Shane Phelan, in her briefer consideration of Sandel and MacIntyre, suggest a related issue. Communitarians have not talked about how to confront the problems, risks, and possibilities associated with introducing (or reintroducing) those who have been treated as "other" into communities.[35] The issue of what has been called "moral communities" is only one empirical problem that has been neglected by communitarian political theorists. Psychologists, philosophers, legal scholars, and others examine (under the rubric of "moral community" or "moral exclusion") how some groups come to be "perceived as *outside the boundary in which moral values, rules, and considerations of fairness apply.*"[36] Assuming that Phelan's concern with the status of lesbians applies equally to members of other—both excluded and dominated— groups, hers is a pressing question for communitarians.

A third criticism offered by Friedman is that there is in communitarianism a subtle bias toward the recognition of some sorts of communities over others. This bias endows some kinds of community with legitimacy when it comes to the role of communities in generating identity, moral claims, and obligations. "Where," she asks, in the writing of communitarians "is the International Ladies Garment Worker's Union, the Teamsters, the Democratic Party, Alcoholics Anonymous, or the Committee in Solidarity with the People of El Salvador?"[37] Where, she might have added, is any understanding of community in which sex/gender itself is an important constitutive element. As Okin points out again and again, contemporary (nonfeminist) theorists of all persuasions fail to notice the ways in which biological sex, gender, and sexual orientation have pervasive moral, legal, social, and political repercussions.

In making a final, "metaphysical," argument about the nature of the self in communitarian philosophy, Friedman notes succinctly that for communitarians "all human selves are constituted by their social and communal relationships."[38] This is an interpretation whose validity has been affirmed already in discussions of the work of Sandel and MacIntyre. It is at the point of such a characterization that the critique of feminist political theorists can be usefully augmented by more psychologically inclined feminists; for feminist psycho-social theories challenge this communitarian identity between the self and the community while retaining many of the insights and concerns advanced by communitarian thought.

The "Communitarian" Self in Feminism

The developing critique of communitarian ideas by feminist political theorists focuses most visibly on inequalities between women and men in communitarian ideals and assumptions. The critique contributes to a variety of dialogues, including that between liberalism and its discontents. Nevertheless, the response of feminist political theorists leaves some areas of interest to feminists better explored than others. In particular, the feminist political theorists do not scrutinize the implicit psychology of communitarianism to see whether the claims of communitarians to have improved upon the account of the self in liberalism are substantiated.

The alarm sounded by feminist political theorists does acknowledge that feminists have found an ally in communitarianism, and some reasons why they might be expected to do so. Communitarians reject a model of the self that leaves it "unsituated"; this is to say that one feature of the rejection of liberalism is the argument that liberals posit an ahistorical self, prior to its relations and commitments. The feminist theorists discussed here would concur in such a rejection, as would many liberals. But further, the feminists develop complex analyses of the sort that liberals have found of little interest: analyses of the interpenetration of social arrangements with identity and of the constitution of the self in and through relations with others.

The communitarians suggest an understanding of the self as much more than a "possessive individualist" and bearer of rational judgment and principles, even if they do not elaborate an account of the self as impassioned. These themes have by now been dominant in feminist interdisciplinary theory for at least two decades. The accounts of the self developed by feminist psycho-social theorists and by communitarian theorists are thus similar in meaningful respects. Both accounts claim to respect and integrate the particularity of the self in its relations with others and to embed the self in history, in discrete social practices, and—in the feminist version—in a gendered body. This promise is fulfilled in some ways, and not in others, in each of the kinds of theory. In general, however, feminist psycho-social theories are more successful and incisive at characterizing the self and its relations with others than communitarian theories.

It might be tempting to conclude that what really separates feminist and communitarian theory, given all their affinities, is the more central and sustained attention in feminist thought to women and women's experience. This would be an accurate characterization. But it is equally true that both traditions of social thought require accounts of the self that integrate the passions.

Unfortunately, in the communitarian account the passions are either absent or become marginalized; direct confrontation with the passions is avoided. A vivid example is the way in which Sandel writes scornfully about the inability of Rawls to conceptualize real selves. In Sandel's view, the Rawlsian self is wraithlike and insubstantial—"a self that seems hardly worth protecting."[39] However, when Sandel tries to make the self more substantial, he does so without reference to the passions. Sandel writes, for example, of the "more or less ideal family" as a realm of "spontaneous affection."[40] Here is one of the few occasions in which the relation between self and world is understood, however abstractly, as imbued with emotion. In terms of Sandel's view of the self, then, it is as though a glimpse inside a—by his own admission—hypothetical family exhausts the potential of his critique to do justice to the passionate and paradoxical nature of human relations. The challenge to a "thin" liberal self is compromised at its root.

In the feminist account, by contrast, the passions are not avoided. Feminist psycho-social theorists, having linked the insistence on the private and nonpolitical nature of feelings with the absence of women and women's concerns in social theory, with reasonable consistency analyze the role of passions in social relations. In Gilligan's theory of women's development, love and care for the self and others is central to morality. For Chodorow, women's greater receptiveness and capacity for abiding emotional connection with others is a consequence of early development. Both Benjamin and Dinnerstein consider domination and inequality features of interpersonal relations that are constructed and manifested through the vicissitudes of the passions.

The problem with the majority of feminist psycho-social theories resides rather in the ways that feminist treatments of the passions have been incomplete. Feminist accounts of the self that integrate agreeable passions without integrating disagreeable ones fail to complete their own transformative vision of selfhood and social relations.

To the extent that feminist psycho-social theorists display many communitarian claims and concerns in constructing their accounts of the self, the feminist account is superior to that provided in communitarianism. This may be in large measure a function of the feminist appropriation and use of psychological paradigms, especially the attempt to address gender difference from the perspective of psychological development. This use of psychology has facilitated a kind of study of the interaction of the passions with social relations that is less likely to be executed by mainstream political theorists.

It is precisely the sophisticated psychology of the feminist account of the self that makes it more compelling than the communitarian account, not just another version of it. When Friedman characterizes the self in communitarian philosophy as "constituted by [its] social and communal relationships" she does not practice much distortion for the sake of simplicity. The most prominent communitarian writings tend to portray the self as the repository of the products of communal life. This self is not an active agent negotiating between psychic demands and an external world of others, although it is, in the often-used phrase, a "socially constituted self."

It is no accident that communitarians construct a supremely socially constituted self. Turning to such an account of the self avoids the perceived liberal errors of imagining the self as prior to the community, or as a bearer of transhistorical reason.[41] The communitarian account, then, at least seriously considers the role of relations with historically and culturally specific others (though not race- and gender-specific others) in the constitution of selves. It fails to inquire deeply enough into this constitution of selves, and it is for this reason that the communitarian alternative to liberal theory is yet too superficial to do justice to its own promises.

By contrast, accounts of the self in feminist psycho-social theories yield more complex and compelling versions of the interaction between self and world than do those of communitarians. It is true that these accounts are not seamless. Feminists have also pursued theoretical visions of the "socially constituted self," and some attempts to articulate this vision have been more successful than others.

Feminist theories tend to handle the integration of the passions more deftly than communitarian theories, yet even they have been, as a group, inconsistent in this regard. This conclusion is most vividly apparent when feminist theories are examined separately. Then it becomes clear that critics of feminism are not the only ones who associate disagreeable passions less closely with women than with men. Feminists themselves, by their silence, often reinforce a stereotype of women's "nature" whose implications for women are mixed.

At their best, theories like those of Gilligan, Chodorow, Benjamin, and Dinnerstein have given feminism a new language of the passions — a new language in which to found knowledge about the dense and resistant reality of the self in relations. Yet as the following chapters demonstrate, these theories are not always at their best when approaching the problem posed by the disagreeable passions.

Conclusion

Feminist theorists are not alone among social and political thinkers in conceptualizing the essentially connected and embedded nature of the self. Feminist psycho-social theories, besides doing many other things, exhibit many of the central concerns of communitarian philosophy, and especially a communitarian account of the self. On the other hand, the continuities and affinities of feminism and communitarianism must not be overestimated. The self in communitarian theory is more abstract, genderless, and psychologically untenable than is frequently supposed. Communitarianism does not seem to be able to support an account of selfhood as impassioned and psychologically defended, even though communitarians often get credit for accommodating such a self through their critique of liberal theory.

It is clear from the gaps that remain in existing critiques of communitarianism in feminist political theory that the foundations of the communitarian self cannot be ignored. Feminist psycho-social accounts of self do manifest many more of the realities of human connection and community than does the communitarian. It is necessary, then, to turn to these theories to give flesh to the skeletal self of communitarianism. In the process, it will be possible to envision especially the female self not only in its loving and empathic relatedness but also in its "disagreeable" variation.

CHAPTER 2

Coming to Terms with the Passions

There is a depth of thought untouched by words, and deeper still a gulf of formless feelings untouched by thought.

—Zora Neale Hurston,
Their Eyes Were Watching God

Reason was failing me—as a lover, mother, and citizen. As Western philosophers had idealized it, Reason was meant to be detached and impersonal, at best irrelevant to particular affections and loyalties. I needed to act on passion and be responsible to love.

—Sara Ruddick,
Maternal Thinking

The Disagreeable Passions in Feminism

It is perhaps ironic to suggest that feminist psycho-social theorists have attended insufficiently to the very passions that stigmatize the women's movement in the public imagination. Feminists are, in fact, described as angry women: women who hate men, or children, or their natural role (or, in the worst scenario, all these). Popular discourse about feminism, thus, situates feminists as demonstrably un- or anti- "feminine." Feminists are spoken of as emotional in ways that constitute them as dark doubles of "real" women; feminism is dangerous in that it sanctions, focuses, and vivifies women's dangerous and disagreeable emotions. Feminists themselves have verified, not the popular verdict, but the role of these passions in their public enterprises.

"It is a tiresome truth of women's experience that our anger is generally not well-received." With this weary understatement, Marilyn Frye begins "A Note on Anger."[1] For Frye, writing of the role of disagreeable emotions in motivating women's revolt necessitates writing of the responses to those emotions. Physical abuse is one response; another is the labeling of angry and embittered women as crazy, insane, "mad."[2] It is an understatement to point out that disagreeable emotions are more frequently punished in women than in men—and have fewer institutionally and culturally approved channels for expression. Women find the expression of rage on behalf of others (children, for example) more socially acceptable than rage exercised on behalf of women in general, or themselves in particular. Women who persist in expressing unwelcome feelings face even the threat of being denied the clearly ascriptive status of "woman," a threat that demonstrates how closely that status is associated with proper behavior and demeanor.

The danger associated with the explicit exposure of these passions in women seems, often to both women and men, to imperil life itself. It is a danger that cannot be tolerated. It is apropos of the response elicited by women's disagreeable feelings that the often satirical *Feminist Dictionary*[3] cross-lists *anger* with *man-hating;* the point is that women's anger is experienced as catastrophic, as that which would kill. The disagreeable passions clearly threaten to disturb natural hierarchies of power. Their absence, however either coerced or illusory, legitimates those hierarchies.

Realizing this, feminist activist-theorists write with passion and clarity about women's hatred and anger. This does not suggest that "feminists," a disparate group, are monolithically impassioned about the same issues, or that they direct these passions in the same ways at the same objects. It is to suggest that feminists have collectively struggled with a need to avow, to acknowledge, the disagreeable passions.

Because feminism is inextricably concerned with political protest, it is not surprising to discover anger and hatred provoked by social and political ills. Racism, sexism, anti-Semitism, state-sanctioned hatred of lesbians and gay men, the waging of war, rape, battering, and other forms of violence against women, the impoverishment of children, class privilege, the despoiling of nature: these are, among many other issues, the objects of feminist rage in contemporary societies.

Whatever their orientation to particular issues and concerns, feminists encounter a bewildering variety of assumptions, from within and without, about the relation of women to the disagreeable passions. It has often been fashionable to suggest that women (including feminist women) simply do not confront negative emotions. It is also assumed (and by feminists themselves) that only in the early years of the "second wave" of feminism were feminists really enraged. In this interpretation, feminists now resist the temptation to vent unfocused and strident wrath and are more reasonable; feminism has become, aside from occasional and unseemly outbursts, agreeable.

Yet if we listen to the voices of feminism today, quite another interpretation presents itself. Feminist thinkers and writers continue to assert the socially transformative nature of women's passions—even, and sometimes especially, the negative ones. This includes women as disparate in other respects as Audre Lorde, Mary Daly, Angela Davis, Andrea Dworkin, and Adrienne Rich, to name but a few. That this aspect of the thought and work of such feminists is not broadly understood as a noteworthy contribution, to feminism or to social thought in general, may be a function of the low esteem in which the exposure of women's disagreeable passions is held.

Consider Audre Lorde's important essay, "The Uses of Anger: Women Responding to Racism." In it Lorde links the conceptual and political work of confronting (personal and social) racism with the capacity to be angry, and to tolerate and use anger. It would no doubt be argued by some readers of the essay that what Lorde is really writing about is racism. But a shift of perspective suggests that she is, in fact, engaging quite a different problem; she is writing about the necessity for women to understand the connections between race hatred and oppression, and their own anger. She locates the "problem" that she addresses neither "in" individual selves, nor "out" in the oppressive world. Instead, the problem is "between"; the breach in the self that mitigates against the recognition and claiming of anger is directly related to the flourishing of other breaches between persons.

In the beginning of the essay Lorde states firmly that she does not "want [the essay] to become a theoretical discussion."[4] To guard against this result she offers vignettes that concretize her arguments about the connections between racism and anger. Nonetheless, the essay is theoretical. Lorde argues that passions are natural and necessary forms of communication within and between persons:

Anger is loaded with information and energy.[5]

When we turn from anger we turn from insight, saying we will accept only the designs already known, deadly and safely familiar. I have tried to learn my anger's usefulness to me, as well as its limitations.[6]

Further, she argues that women's disagreeable passions, in particular, have been muted, perverted, and silenced, often by women themselves:

Any discussion among women about racism must include the recognition and the use of anger. This discussion must be direct and creative because it is crucial. We cannot allow our fear of anger to deflect us nor seduce us into settling for anything less than the hard work of excavating honesty.[7]

In characterizing, and criticizing, homogeneous white women's consciousness raising groups, Lorde says, "There was work on expressing anger, but very little on anger directed against each other. No tools were developed to deal with other women's anger except to avoid it, deflect it, or flee from it under a blanket of guilt."[8] Lorde concludes that, in spite of the urgent need to do so, "most women have not developed tools for facing anger constructively."[9]

What is interesting about this feminist account of anger is that it focuses not on the hatred or malevolent acts of oppressors. Instead, Lorde challenges feminist women to excavate, comprehend, and use their own anger—this in order that maiming social evils might be redressed. Lorde's essay on anger is one that suggests the deliberate use of anger; by contrast, in the work of Andrea Dworkin rage is inscribed in the texts. Exemplary is Dworkin's book *Intercourse*. As early as 1978 Dworkin had written, on the subject of pornography and violence against women, that her own anger had yielded to "grief."[10] Perhaps, but this description does not account for the relentless, irrepressibly enraged quality of Dworkin's prose. In Dworkin's texts to a greater extent than many other feminist texts, rage in response to harm is neither subverted, denied, rationalized, nor sublimated. The threat of female anger and menace intrinsic to both subject matter and narrative voice is retained intact.

The passion in Dworkin's writing is, broadly, in the service of identifying and combating violence against women in its multiple manifestations—what she called in an early work "woman hating." Feminists like Dworkin have effectively used the disagreeable emotions as political or as psychological tools. But the passions are not only expedient means to agendas of social and individual psychological transformation. They are essential to feminist theory. The theoretical neglect of emotions that are regarded as undesirable, especially when their undesirability mirrors a social repugnance of their appearance in women, contributes to invisibility. The passions and the role that they play in human experience are made invisible, and so, as a consequence, are women and their projects.

Conceptualizing and integrating the disagreeable passions is necessary for feminist theory. To account for the full range of emotions in feminist theories of selfhood challenges notions of women as fully subjected. Such accounts are essential to theories of autonomy in social relations. The actual truncation of the passions has also been associated with adult moral incapacity. A full theory of moral and political agency would require speaking not only of the loving but also of the hating of the self. One way to reintegrate these passions into contemporary feminist thinking is to do as many feminist theorists have already done: make use of psychoanalytic object relations theory.

Early Object Relations Theory

There have been many, often conflicting, definitions of "object relations" and the kind of theory it denotes. It is, therefore, useful to consider the definitions employed by object relations analysts and thinkers themselves. In this respect, the thought of Melanie Klein and Donald Winnicott, called by one recent theorist "the two most prominent founding figures" of object relations theory, is central.[11] Feminist social theorists, already regarded as revisionists of Freud, also rely upon and revise the ideas of these early object relations thinkers.

Klein, and "Kleinian" thinkers in general, have been credited by many scholars of psychoanalytic thought with having extended Freud's concept of internal objects (and phantasy).[12] They are understood as having helped to create the foundation for a new way of conceptualizing psychic life not dependent on Freud's conception of "drives." Such a reconceptualization is valuable, but not because Freud ignored the passions. It is more that he subordinated the passions to innate drives (or "instincts") that he assumed "to lie in the biological body and the genetic inheritance expressed in bodily development."[13] Many shortcomings of drive theory have been established by critics. Feminists have noted particularly that to conceptualize persons as receptacles for—even if simultaneously shapers of—drives is to circumscribe the nature of human connection. It is to make affiliation entirely derivative of the need for drive satisfaction. And this position is theoretically, as well as phenomenologically, inadequate.

What, then, is meant by "object relations"? This paradigm is generally regarded as being predicated upon certain assumptions derived from analytic practice: that unconscious phantasy is the natural and constant constituent of mental life;[14] that the character of internal "objects" is constructed from experience—mediated and shaped by bodily needs, anxieties, defenses, and developmental capacities;[15] that phantasies of connections, dialogues, or relations among objects help to structure modes of relating with the self and with real, external others.

The language of object relations theory is sometimes criticized for its (misleading) assimilation of spatial and concrete images.[16] However perceptive this criticism, object relations ideas do convey the literalness of much internal experience. An additional complication is that the term *object* refers sometimes to the internal experience, and sometimes to the external person. Although feminist object relations tends to be more systematic in its identification of "object" with "person," object relations proper maintains this more capacious definition. Its usefulness is in stressing the mutually constitutive nature of inner and outer reality.

Some critics of object relations thought have claimed that there is an essential inwardness, an exclusive intrapsychic focus, that makes object relations inappropriate for social or political theorizing. Object relations does not address the relations among people, according to this view; it addresses only what are necessarily private worlds.

There is certainly support for this interpretation in object relations theory. Klein herself is, as Greenberg and Mitchell note, often misunderstood as one who "neglects the importance of real people altogether at the expense of fantastic and phantasmogoric creations of the child's own mind."[17] But there is another perspective on this debate that refocuses the criticism of isolated (apolitical) individuality in a more fruitful way. This is that object relations theory, through its focus on intrapsychic processes, grasps the ways in which meaning in external reality is constantly in the process of being created by the self.

Thomas Ogden recognizes this constitutive aspect of intrapsychic life. In Ogden's view, it is internal processes of the sort described by Klein and Winnicott that "generate meaning and experience."[18] This is, in fact, what object relations achieves: It provides tools with which to theorize about how "internal" processes shape the acquisition and character of "external" reality and how, in turn, that reality affects the nature of the self.[19]

Consistent with this perspective is an interpretation that understands neither "internal objects" nor "phantasy" as the real content of object relations theory. C. Fred Alford argues that what Kleinian theory, in particular, yields is an understanding of the self as impassioned:

If objects are not primary, neither are the phantasies that are about them. The passions are primary. It is love and hate, and all their combinations and permutations, that generate and motivate unconscious phantasy.[20]

The social-theoretical implication of Klein's thought is not a socially-constituted self, but a self understood as the locus of the passions of love and hate, immediately experienced by the self and mediately related to others.[21]

Reading Kleinian theory—or, more broadly, object relations theory— in this way is a choice. But it is a choice that is consistent with Klein's own concentration on emotional vicissitudes, for example, in her foundational accounts of envy and love. Donald Meltzer suggests that Klein's "expansion" of Freudian theory advanced psychoanalytic understanding in two critical areas: emotionality and internal life. In Meltzer's view, it is Klein's contribution to psychoanalytic theory "that we do not live in one world, but in two—that we live in an internal world which is as real a place to live in as the outside world."[22]

So to take object relations thought seriously is to take seriously the impact of internal life and the passions on the self and on society. In differing ways and to differing degrees, this is what feminist object relations theorists do. They do not accomplish this by incorporating every aspect of object relations theory; indeed, given the vastness of the literature, this would be impossible. Feminists who use object relations thought have, for example, deliberately excised sexist conclusions and speculations regarding gender roles and female "nature." For all this, however, the debate over an accommodation between feminist theory and object relations theory rages.

Feminism against Object Relations

The feminist appropriation of object relations theory has not been without its feminist critics. Just as some feminists have constructed elegant theories of gender identity and relations using object relations perspectives, others have found object relations (and often psychoanalysis generally) to be deeply flawed. These critics do not merely suggest that object relations might be more incisively used to address problems such as the silence of theory on the subject of aggression and rage. They frequently reject its appropriation by feminists altogether. Because the argument of the following chapters is that the appropriation of object relations theory is useful to feminist theory, it is worthwhile to examine these counterclaims and arguments.

First, object relations theory is said to privilege characteristics or qualities of selfhood such as separation and individuation, or to create a normative discourse that promotes depersonalization or abstraction from relation with others. This is a charge made by Carol Gilligan in evaluating the work of Nancy Chodorow. In a polemical mood, Pauline Bart criticizes object relations thought (again, as it is employed by Chodorow): "For those not familiar with object relations theory, the first thing to understand is that *people are called objects.*"[23] Sara Ruddick calls the kind of selfhood presumed, and enforced, by object relations "abstract masculinity." By this she means, as other writers also argue, that within object relations theory is embedded a teleological end of "distance" from others associated, as feminists have demonstrated, with ideal adult (read *male*) development.[24]

One of the most thorough accounts of the inadequacy of object relations for feminism is that of Judith Kegan Gardiner. In "Self-Psychology as Feminist Theory" Gardiner cites the failure of object relations to accommodate developmental modes that diverge from a model of separation. "Object relations theorists like Margaret Mahler," she writes, "chart infant developmental growth as a progress from 'symbiosis' with the mother to independence, autonomy, individuation."[25] The attribution to Mahler (and a few others) of exemplary object relations status plagues many critiques of object relations theory. In fact, Mahler is more generally regarded by scholars of psychoanalytic history as working within the tradition of ego psychology. This does not deny that there are object relational elements in the work of theorists like Mahler, but it does make problematic the rejection of object relations theory on this basis.

Second, object relations is seen as a universalizing discourse, one that masks social and historical particularity, and that is unable to accommodate differences of race and class. Gilligan has advanced the charge that the unself-conscious use of singular categories—"the mother" and "the child"—is a clue to the way in which object relations cloaks the real diversity behind the ostensibly neutral descriptions.[26] Ruddick argues that psychoanalytic object relations theory is contaminated by "patriarchal values" in ways that practitioners do not admit.[27] This can be understood as related to the claim of a universalizing discourse in that object relations assumes a certain "generic" self that is, in fact, white and male; those outside of this implicit "model" of selfhood are marginalized or disappear from the discourse. Elizabeth Fee argues that

object relations theory . . . is based on modern, Western, nuclear families within capitalist societies—and it essentially concerns families in which an isolated full-time mother takes direct responsibility for child-care and housework, while the absent father is occupied in the labor market. The tendency, however, is to suppose that the sex-gender system with which we are most familiar remains, at least in essentials, always and everywhere the same.[28]

For all these reasons, Elizabeth Fee indicates that it is impossible for object relations theory to account for persons who are not represented within the theory itself. Experiences foreign to the theory can only be translated into the already theorized possibilities, creating a situation in which all persons are measured against the "norm" and most are found wanting.

Gardiner also makes this argument in her defense of psychoanalytic self-psychology. It is, however, Elizabeth Spelman's version of this criticism that is unusual for its incisiveness. Spelman is one of few critics who unambiguously focuses not on object relations thought in general but on its adaptation by Nancy Chodorow, and especially on the troubling absence of analysis that would systematically link race and class with gender issues in identity.[29] It is not Spelman's purpose to suggest that other versions of object relations theory might correct the inadequacies that she finds in Chodorow's work, but other feminists suggest this possibility. Jean Grimshaw observes that object relations theory can be employed by feminists to create theories that explain the psychic consequences of changing social forms.[30] In a similar vein, Jane Flax argues that it is the very "logic" of object relations theory that accounts for changes in "human nature . . . as social relations change."[31]

A third criticism of object relations is that it, like its orthodox forebear, is said either to cast a punitive eye on the mother as "bad" or view her solely as a dehumanized mirror of the child. Sometimes these claims are combined: "Object relations theory focuses on the mother as noxious influence. Mothers are experienced solely as objects who do or do not live up to their children's expectations."[32] Not only are object relations theorists represented as mother blaming; more important, the theoretical system itself is said to be inexorable in providing no other way for mothers to be represented. Expression is sometimes given to this criticism in the following way: The shift from object relations theory to feminist object relations theory is positive in that it confounds and corrects for the tendency to blame mother.

A focus on the primacy of the mother's role in ego-formation is not in itself new. It follows upon the attempts of theorists such as Melanie Klein, Michael and Alice Balint, John Bowlby, and Margaret Mahler to cast light on that dim psychic region which Freud likened to the Minoan civilization preceding the Greek. . . . What distinguishes feminist accounts of the mother-child relationship from those in the mainstream of psychoanalytic thought, however, is that they see it from the mother's rather than the child's point of view.[33]

Object relations theory is credited with pushing back the Freudian perspective on development to an earlier moment in the life cycle. But in so doing, object relations theorists make the mother responsible for every evil. Feminists (like Chodorow), it is then conceded, reconnoiter the territory of early childhood and assume the perspective of the mother, in this sense if in no other performing a positive service. But this is generally an unintended compliment, and does not detract from the larger complaint.

Other less frequently encountered claims are no less disparaging. Some critics claim that feminist uses of object relations theory do not accomplish the explanatory ends claimed by theorists; specifically they do not explain the roots of masculine domination, though they may explain some aspects of the perpetuation of domination.[34] Often feminist object relations theorists do not make grand claims of issuing a final explanation for patriarchy. Even if they, or other, theorists make this claim, however, a rejection of their work premised entirely on the failure to discover the cause of patriarchy is premature.

Another criticism suggests that object relations is inherently constrained in its scope by its emphasis on infantile life; it needlessly assumes the hegemony of childhood psychic life over later development. Gardiner's claim, consistent with her thesis, is that self-psychology is more sensitive to life-span and social issues, and is therefore superior to object relations as a paradigm for studying women's lives.[35] Another example is Alice Rossi's startling claim that much of Chodorow's work is unimportant because the impact of infancy and early childhood is obliterated by later "hormonal events and physical changes in puberty."[36] Chodorow's trenchant reply is that if this is so, concern about optimal infant care would be moot; early experience would leave no trace.[37]

Some critics charge that object relations endows fantasy (intrapsychic life) with more significance than reality (life as it is lived with others). The context of this rejection is the position that the preoccupation on the part of feminists with intrapsychic phenomena deflects attention from the world of women's economic exploitation, physical oppression, material want, and historical activity. Ruth Perry paraphrases the concerns of these feminists when she asks, in her review of Chodorow's *Feminism and Psychoanalytic Theory*, "Why read about Freud and object relations theory when real problems stalk the earth?" Perry answers that

by exploring the primal experience of growing up in a family, psychoanalytic theory can account for . . . how a culturally constructed sex/gender system takes hold in the unconscious, showing itself in intractable emotional responses or retrograde erotic fantasies that no amount of rational analysis can eradicate.[38]

The argument that a preoccupation with inner life is politically regressive in fact provides a common reason for rejecting all varieties of psychoanalytic thought, not just object relations theory. It is only due to the fame and influence of particular feminist uses of object relations that the argument can be taken as a critique of object relations.

A final concern that bears expression can be related to post-modern theories of all description. These cast doubt on the legitimacy of claims for transhistorical aspects of identity or subjectivity. If object relations theorists posit, either explicitly or implicitly, the existence of fixed qualities in human beings as the objects of psychoanalytic knowledge and discourse, they are vulnerable to post-modern skepticism and deconstruction. Of course, feminists would raise additional questions about the ways in which such fixed qualities were represented as sexed.

In addressing this potential question about object relations theory, Jane Flax argues that theorists do make one essentialist claim. This is "that human beings by nature are 'object seeking' in the sense of coming into the world equipped for and requiring "sociability." [39] Neither Klein, Winnicott, nor other object relations theorists assume that sociability proceeds in predetermined ways toward predictable outcomes; certainly none would assume that sociability is without disruption, discontinuity, or profound originality. After all, there is no unproblematic mirroring or absorption of the world in the psyche.

One problem with the charge of essentialism is that it is ambiguous enough that large numbers of feminist theorists of all persuasions have at one time or another stood so accused. Another problem is that although charges of essentialism play a critical role in forcing reconsideration of grand statements about the nature of persons, such charges can also inhibit theorizing. Janet Montefiore points out (with reference to criticisms of Nancy Chodorow) that "anti-essentialism has now hardened into an unhelpful orthodoxy" that inhibits disagreement among competing theoretic paradigms. [40]

It is possible to respond to all these criticisms in ways that preserve the usefulness of object relations theory for feminism. The claims just enumerated can be addressed in two different ways: Some are predicated on misunderstandings of object relations theory; others reflect accurate assessments of object relations theory which, at the same time, do not deal mortal wounds to the usefulness of object relations for feminist theory. The critique of the disagreeable passions that guides this argument fulfills several criteria: It is consistent with early object relations theory; it challenges the adequacy of the foregoing criticisms; it is amenable to the uses to which object relations theory has already been put by the majority of feminist thinkers under consideration. First, however, it is necessary to move from the general realm of object relations to the more particular thinkers whose ideas form the basis of this critique.

Melanie Klein

The ideas of Melanie Klein have frequently been peremptorily dismissed by feminists, and even by psychoanalytically oriented feminists. This lack of interest can be attributed to one or more of the following characteristics imputed to her: a nearly exclusive emphasis on aggression as the source of human motivation, status as a drive theorist, and neglect of external reality.[41] As readings of Klein's work, none of these criticisms is entirely unfounded. Klein does impute a generous share of destructive and aggressive desire to the infant and, by extension, to the adult; she did regard her thought to be continuous with Freud's in the conceptualization of the drives;[42] she was often unconcerned with aspects of real relationships and their consequences for psychic life. As a result of the partial validity of such criticisms as these, Klein's work has been read as less contradictory and complex than it actually is.

There continues to be a great deal of difference of opinion, among feminists and nonfeminists alike, about how to situate Klein. She has been characterized as a "psychoanalyst of the passions" by one political theorist, who means by this that Klein derives from the directionless biological drives of Freudian theory intrinsically social and relational passions as the motive force of human feeling and action.[43] Jay Greenberg and Stephen Mitchell, in an attempt to convey the extent of Klein's substantial revision of Freud, argue that *"drives, for Klein, are relationships."*[44] Juliet Mitchell elaborates on this connection:

Klein developed a model of mental development which she amended and amplified throughout her life. Simplifying somewhat, I would suggest that Klein's basic model is that the neonate brings into the world two main conflicting impulses: love and hate. . . . love is the manifestation of the life drive; hate, destructiveness and envy are emanations of the death drive. . . . Furthermore, the baby encounters a world which is both satisfying and frustrating. It exists from the start in a relationship with another person or part of that person.[45]

The issue of whether to regard Klein as merely another drive theorist or as a thinker more amenable to the complexities and exigencies of relational life cannot be settled easily in favor of the former. It is true that Klein is difficult to typify for many reasons. Her idiosyncratic uses of psychoanalytic terms and concepts and her sometimes unpersuasive clinical disquisitions are two of these. In spite of these issues, however, Kleinian theory has much to offer to students of social relations.

Throughout Klein's written works the theme of the vicissitudes of emotions—of love, hate, rage, gratitude, guilt, jealousy, envy, affection—is paramount. Relations, both within the self and among selves, provide the medium for the exploration of these emotions, and are valued for their own sake. Klein constructs a conceptual map on which to trace the psychic development of the self through the passions and the relationships that give them form.

Donald Winnicott

Donald Winnicott, a colleague of Klein's in the British Psychoanalytic Society, was frequently identified with the Kleinian "school," although he often diverged from Klein. Reviews by feminist theorists of Winnicott's contribution to an understanding of human development have been mixed: some note the centrality in his work of the concept of the "mirroring" role of the mother and argue that this and other aspects of his treatment of mothers deny subjectivity to women; others note a demeaning or condescending tone when he addresses the mothering "experts" who are nonetheless the objects of his tutelage.[46] Generally, however, Winnicott's work tends to be favored by feminists (including Carol Gilligan, Nancy Chodorow, and Jessica Benjamin); Dorothy Dinnerstein, whose work will be addressed in chapter 5, is an exception to this preference.

What accounts for the partiality extended to Winnicott by many feminist theorists? There are two explanations: First, Winnicott is attractive to feminist theorists, who seek to ameliorate the social sources of women's distress and oppression, in his consistent attention to the social reality beyond the self—both in the mother-child dyad and in surrounding relationships; second, he disputes with such of Klein's formulations as the "death instinct" and thus appears to mitigate her conviction of the inevitability of hatred, aggression, and destructiveness.

Winnicott was aware that the concern he evinced for the interpersonal reality of his analysands was a departure from Klein's primary interest in the internal dynamics of the self. Indeed, he expressed exasperation with Klein's ostensible lack of commitment to studying the "social":

My trouble when I start to speak to Melanie about her statement of early infancy is that I feel as if I were talking about colour to the colour-blind. She simply says that she has not forgotten the mother and the part the mother plays, but in fact I find that she has shown no evidence of understanding the part the mother plays at the very beginning.[47]

What is perhaps less frequently noticed is the particular way in which Winnicott's lauded interest in the causative—and meliorative—dimension of interpersonal experience is a double-edged sword for feminists. His conviction that the quality of "holding," or care, that the infant and child receive is definitive in shaping development is connected with his focus on the role of the mother as external world, the mother as "maternal environment." This phrase refers at one and the same time to the critical function of mothering—that which Klein is accused of ignoring—while masking the assumption that Winnicott shares with countless other theorists and "experts": that child care not only is but ought to be performed by females. In other words, within Winnicott's scrupulous attention to the interaction between self and world is embedded a belief in sole maternal care and a perhaps inadvertent propensity toward "mother-blaming."[48]

There remains the necessity of examining what seems to be Winnicott's lesser emphasis on hatred and aggression. Because Winnicott is widely understood to be a theorist who disputes with Klein over the innateness of the aggressive drive, he can be understood as one who qualifies and marginalizes the role of these disagreeable passions altogether. On the contrary, Winnicott challenged much about the Kleinian account of these passions, but he never questioned their centrality in psychic and social life. He hailed Klein's "depressive position" as her "most important achievement":[49] "Klein takes up the idea of the destructiveness of the baby and gives it proper emphasis, at the same time making a new and vital issue out of the idea of the fusion of erotic and destructive impulses as a sign of health."[50] In Adam Phillips's words, Winnicott concludes that "it is . . . only through the aggressive component that relationship with real others can exist."[51] The attraction to

Winnicott within feminist psycho-social theory is explicable, but it becomes so through comparison with what is avoided—the thought of Klein. Hence, Winnicott's ideas will be taken up in the chapters that follow, singularly and in comparison with Klein's.

The Feminist Appropriation of Object Relations

Feminism and psychoanalysis have a history that is decades long and complicated. This is, in part, a function of the schisms and divergences that characterize each of these as independent modes of thought. Feminism has always been rent by internal divisions over goals, philosophies, and methods, making it more responsible and accurate to speak as many do of the plural, "feminisms."

Some feminists have attempted to claim for women the promises of the Enlightenment: reason, liberty, autonomy, equality. Others have used psychoanalytic theory to expose these claims and promises as incoherent, or as the residue of unexamined forms of domination. Neither has the integration of psychoanalytic theories with feminism been unproblematic. The diverse traditions within psychoanalytic thought have been credited variously with contributing to women's oppression and with delivering the means of exposing oppression and ameliorating it.

The appropriation of aspects of the psychoanalytic tradition known as "object relations" by feminists is among feminism's most recent and influential developments. As we have seen already, this development is one that remains contested. In spite of this, however, feminists have made use of object relations ideas in many contexts: from the study of the acquisition of gender identity to the nature of scientific inquiry.[52] In what ways have feminist social theorists integrated object relations?

Janet Sayers argues that feminist social theory has been influenced, perhaps unwittingly, by the work of analyst Melanie Klein in two ways: in its positive treatment of female sexuality and its emphasis on mothering. Yet even Sayers's characterization of Klein is ambiguous: in one work[53] she argues that feminist social theorists have borrowed from Kleinian theory to construct their accounts of female sexuality and mothering, whereas in another[54] she makes "Kleinian" theory and object relations theory distinct. In the latter, Sayers does not address, and thus does not refute, the more usual recognition of Klein as an object relations theorist.[55]

This exclusion of Klein from the category of object relations theory is not theoretically useful. It is more accurate to claim that feminists have overcome limitations of Freudian thought by selectively appropriating from the discourse of object relations theory, including—and excluding—aspects of the thought of Klein and other early object relations theorists. It is true that on both the subject of female sexuality and the psychological centrality of the mothering relation feminists have found traditional psychoanalytic theory inadequate. Yet these are not the only ways in which feminists have made use of object relations theories.

Feminists have, in fact, employed object relations perspectives toward three additional ends: first, to demonstrate the ways in which identity is constructed in relation to others, against drive theory; second, to assert the fundamental and irreducible need for relatedness in selves so constructed; and third, to demonstrate the existence of moral and political autonomy, especially in women. Not all the feminist social theorists whose work is grounded in some version of psychological theory self-consciously pursue these objectives. However, when taken collectively, the feminist object relations literature can be read to pursue these ends. As a whole this literature constitutes a significant challenge to other modern philosophic notions of selfhood, and to various politics of exclusion.

Feminist object relations theorists renounce the anomic vision of the self in Freudian psychoanalytic thought. Nancy Chodorow argues in "Beyond Drive Theory" that object relations theory provides a good foundation for critical social theory partly because it shifts emphasis away from Freudian drives and repression.[56] Rather than the self as a bearer of drives, a seeker of gratification from the outside world, these feminists envision a self fundamentally connected to others. They argue, in the face of dissent from other feminists, that object relations offers a way of theorizing sources of human connection.

A definitional issue is elemental to this debate about the relational nature of selfhood in object relations. In the same ways that object relations feminists borrow selectively from early object relations thought, so too do critics categorize theorists selectively. Critics thus present as exemplary of object relations theory the ideas of those whom they have classed as object relations theorists. In this way, Margaret Mahler, to name one prominent example, is classified by such critics of object relations as Gilligan and Gardiner as a central object relations theorist;

Mahler's work on "separation" and "individuation" in child development is then read as typical of an object relations insistence on independent, unconnected selfhood.[57]

However accurate this assessment of Mahler's work is (and there are ways in which its subtleties are unappreciated), the real question is begged. Can Margaret Mahler or John Bowlby, another similarly treated figure, be regarded as paradigmatic theorists of object relations? The answer is no, even though both Mahler and Bowlby, as well as numerous others, fashion their psychoanalytic theories with obvious object relational elements. Much of the confusion about which theorists, works, and ideas can be read to express what is definitive about object relations is also found in feminist object relations. In particular, the hesitancy among feminists to recognize Melanie Klein as a founding object relations thinker is of interest.

With few exceptions, feminists do not employ Klein's thought.[58] Sometimes her position in the history of psychoanalytic theory is ignored altogether; other times she is mentioned briefly or excluded from the category of object relations theorists. This is curious, because nonfeminist accounts of object relations theory, and of psychoanalytic theory, make her work prominent.[59] If Sayers is correct in her conclusion that Klein's ideas, or their progeny, have found their way into feminist discourse, it appears inconsistent that Klein has not. The inconsistency of identification of object relations thinkers is a meaningful one for understanding the feminist appropriation of object relations.

Sayers argues that although feminists have utilized object relations perspectives in creating broader social theories, in one area these feminists have failed to incorporate completely the insights of object relations. Rage and aggression are, she argues, inadequately conceptualized by much feminist theory.[60] Yet, a "focus on the place of aggression and rage in mental life," rejected or ignored by feminists, is available in Kleinian theory. Simply put, disagreeable emotions must be studied by feminists because

aggression poses a peculiar problem to oppressed groups in society. Not only are they more frequently its victims, but they are also often regarded as essentially lacking in aggression.[61]

Klein's work is relevant to feminism for, more than any of the other early psychoanalysts, she draws attention to the hatred (as well as the love) that characterizes the infant's relation to its mother. And, in doing this, her work serves as an important corrective to recent feminist celebrations of the mother-infant relation as a "lost paradise of mutual affection" between women.[62]

Sayers's insight about this silence in feminist psychoanalytic social theory is perspicacious. Unfortunately, she pursues the insight unevenly.[63] Because Sayers does not understand Klein as an object relations theorist, she remains unable to conceptualize Kleinian ideas in the context either of the ideas of other object relations thinkers or of different interpretations. The consequence is that many of the nuances of Klein's ideas, including some internal contradictions, are prematurely resolved in the service of Sayers's political agenda. In criticizing the silence in feminist theory around the disagreeable passions, Sayers's conclusions are disconcertingly inconsistent.

The most important respect in which this is true can be found in Sayers's simultaneous claims that oppression and social subordination "produce" anger and rage in women, and that these circumstances "evoke" these emotions.[64] Without challenging what Sayers concludes about the social position of women, it is possible to rebut the position that she (again, inconsistently) adopts on the source of disagreeable emotions: that they can be understood exclusively as products of the experience of social injustice by women, and are then, presumably, entirely remediable.

Such a position is not merely incommensurable with an object relations perspective; it is inconsistent with Sayers's own presentation of the complexity of relationships. Most glaringly it is at odds with her analysis of the distorted nature of many feminist accounts of the mother-child relation. Sayers cites Klein as the theorist who most credibly accounts for the contradictions of internal feeling, first in the "original" relation, and finally, in later relations. She criticizes Gilligan, Chodorow, Benjamin, and Dinnerstein, as well as Adrienne Rich, Juliet Mitchell, and Luce Irigaray, for presenting an unconflictedly loving version of women's relations.[65] Yet, in spite of this, women's anger, rage, and aggression come, in Sayers's work, to be understood as the products of patriarchal relations.

To be sure, this deficiency in perspective is not entirely ignored by feminist theorists. Jane Flax warns feminists against attributing women's negative feelings, "women's rage or depression," entirely to "external society."[66] The feminist slogan Women Are Not Mad, They Are Angry is useful, but it can be misleading if all disagreeable feelings come to be accounted as the conscious consequence of oppression. Flax, like Sayers, argues that feminists often "avoid discussing women's anger and aggression." Flax places this criticism in the context of what she understands as a dichotomizing tendency in social theory: the opposition of "autonomy to being-in-relation."[67] Being-in-relation, as Flax notes, is inherently paradoxical: connection can be aggressive, claustrophobic, destructive—and still be connection. Feminist theory has not always adequately acknowledged this complexity.

Sayers does accurately advise of Klein's lack of attention to social relations of subordination and violence. And Sayers's criticisms of feminist theory are incisive. But her attempt at an integration of Kleinian ideas ends by being primarily suggestive of a direction for further investigation, rather than conclusive. The exclusion of Kleinian theory from feminist thought remains largely unanalyzed even after it is remarked on by Sayers.

Interestingly, this same gap appears in an essay by Toril Moi. Moi contends that a denunciation of aggression in feminist theory is misconceived. She criticizes the "non-Kleinian object-relations theory" of Nancy Chodorow for its "failure to theorize resistance, disruption, and failure of identity." Such feminist theory, she argues, "does not take the unconscious sufficiently into account."[68] Moi remarks in a footnote that Chodorow's variety of object relations theory is prey to certain epistemological difficulties. It "stress[es] adaptation as an aim of psychoanalysis, privilege[s] external reality, and neglect[s] psychical reality. [It] discount[s] Klein's theory because it is not based on external reality."[69]

Despite this criticism, however, Moi does not suggest that Kleinian theory be integrated into feminist object relations or feminist social theory in general as a possible corrective to the problems she perceives. She instead introduces a feminist reappraisal of Freudian theory that, although useful to her analysis, leaves aside the question of Klein that she raises: Would the appropriation of relatively underutilized perspectives from early object relations thought be useful to feminism, and if so, how?

Conclusion

Disagreeable passions, in all their permutations, are a feature of social and political life. Feminism, as theoretical discourse and political movement, has responded to the passions in very different ways. Feminists have sometimes responded with silence or denial; but feminists have also claimed disagreeable passions, used them, and tried to account for their tenacity in social and intimate relations.

The most prominent feminist psycho-social theories give divergent expression to disagreeable passions, especially in women. These feminist theorists also favor Donald Winnicott over Melanie Klein as a progenitor of object relations theory. Melanie Klein has been accused of ignoring, or being unaware of, the external world and the significance of its human diversity. Yet she and others initiated clinical and theoretical work that is, in its structure, amenable to the exploration and affirmation of social relations. These tools are useful to feminism; one example of their application is in the study of the disagreeable passions in feminist social theory.

Doubtless the most famous of all feminist psycho-social theories is Carol Gilligan's theory of women's moral development. The following chapter subjects Gilligan's theory to a unique critique that exposes her avoidance of the disagreeable passions through comparison with the moral-developmental arguments and observations of Klein and Winnicott.

The Voices of Care
and Reparation

to have
and not to hold, to love
with minimized malice, hunger
and anger moment by moment balanced.
— Marge Piercy,
"To Have without Holding"

The Care Perspective

The relational psychology pioneered by Carol Gilligan and her associates
has emerged as a challenge to liberal and realist theories of society. This
challenge is founded upon a vision of women as inextricably connected
to others in their deepest commitments, beliefs, ideals, judgments, and
actions. The affinities between Gilligan's female self and the self constructed by the communitarians is obvious to students of political
thought. What is less obvious is the fact that Gilligan's account is a
partial one in which the field of "relation" is circumscribed from the
outset. In order to understand how this is so it is necessary to draw out
the implications of Gilligan's ideas, including her conversation with
Lawrence Kohlberg, the place of emotions in moral life, the often contested role of gender in her theory, and her responses to psychoanalytic
theory.

Since the late 1970s Gilligan and her colleagues have produced an influential and controversial account of moral life, "a different voice" than that generally heard and acknowledged by psychologists and philosophers. It has been Gilligan's project to rectify the exclusion of women, and women's experience and perspectives, from the moral domain. On the basis of her empirical research with diverse samples of subjects, Gilligan concludes that a style of moral development and response, in fact of moral perception itself, has been consistently overlooked. This style is associated with care and a recognition of the priority of relationships; it is argued to be virtually exclusively practiced by women.

In Gilligan's theory, the stages[1] through which women develop are: first, an egocentric stage of care for the self; second, a selfless stage of care for and concern about the other; and finally, a stage in which care for self and other are balanced and integrated.[2] In her more recent work with adolescent girls Gilligan does deemphasize the characteristics of developmental stages. She suggests through her interview interpretations that "stages" do not neatly supersede one another, but rather provide differing strategies by means of which particular dilemmas can be resolved.[3]

Gilligan's theory can be usefully read as a theory about gender difference (although this reading has precipitated much of the controversy that surrounds it). It can also, however, be read as a challenge to hegemonic versions of moral selfhood in psychology and moral and political philosophy. The ethic of care that Gilligan discovers and elaborates presents an account of the moral self that recognizes that self as essentially connected to others. In Gilligan's account the self is "thick"—constituted of particular relationships and characteristics, including cognitive and affective dispositions.[4] This interpersonal perspective presupposes the salience of both reason and emotion in moral responsiveness; the focus is on whole persons and the relations between persons, not interactions between noumenal selves or bundles of rights.

The aspects of the ethic of care that are most relevant to the present discussion are: first, the way in which it encourages a conceptualization of moral life as inextricably connected with emotional capacities and processes; and second, the nature of its similarities and differences with a Kleinian moral theory. Love, care, and empathy are not exclusively descriptions of private affect for Gilligan but are the names of processes by which persons engage in relationships and resolve moral dilemmas.

Emotions of love and empathy are, for Gilligan as for object relations theorists, inherently interpersonal; they are precipitates of relations and enable individuals to endow the external world with significance.

There is, however, a set of emotions to which Gilligan ascribes far less significance for the human enterprise of moral response and meaning making. The virtual absence of the disagreeable passion from Gilligan's theory makes it a "sanguine vision."[5] This absence also ultimately prevents some insights about moral life that are not inconsistent with Gilligan's larger theoretical purpose.

In *In a Different Voice* Gilligan rejects a Freudian psychoanalytic contribution to a theory of women's moral identity. In other writings she is equally critical of other psychoanalytic theories. Yet it is not the case that all psychoanalytic perspectives on the evolution and dynamics of moral response stand in opposition to Gilligan's. The object relational approach to moral theory developed by Melanie Klein, and extended by Donald Winnicott, is similar in many respects to the ethic of care. Perhaps even more than Gilligan, Klein offers a model of moral selfhood that is sensitive to the interaction between internal and external worlds, especially the ways in which psychic processes are used to create meaning in the world of relations with others.

A Kleinian moral theory, although it does not focus on the gendered nature of morality, discloses love and care for others as the core of moral life. Equally central, however, is the role of hatred and psychic aggression. It is here that the accounts of Gilligan and Klein diverge. For Klein, psychic life is a complex and passionate struggle of conflicting emotions; hatred and love vie with each other in explicable patterns and processes.

In order to examine more closely the similarities and differences in these two theories, Gilligan's theory is considered first, with particular attention to the role of emotion in her account of morality. Next, criticisms of her work that focus on the relative absence of disagreeable passions are presented. Finally, aspects of Klein's moral theory that reveal the interconnections between agreeable and disagreeable passions are delineated, making possible a final comparison between the two theorists.

Thinking and Feeling

Gilligan's theory was originally a response to Lawrence Kohlberg's theory of moral development. Kohlberg's theory has been subjected to a wide variety of criticisms, one of which focuses on the exclusively cognitive basis of that theory.[6] Kohlberg has argued, after Kant and much (though not all) of the liberal philosophical tradition, that moral theories must be universalizable and address the cognitive capacities of persons. Seyla Benhabib, in citing the conclusions of Kohlberg as "distortingly cognitivistic," argues that the cognitive-developmental paradigm "ignores the role of affects" in the construction of the self.[7]

On this reading of Kohlberg's moral theory, a principal contribution of Gilligan's thought has been to challenge the dichotomy that Kohlberg frequently assumes between the public/moral domain of human interchange and the private/intimate domain of personal relationships. In the latter, for Kohlberg, considerations of moral judgment and action proper do not intrude.[8] The fact that a conceptual division between "public" and "private" has consistently corresponded to a division between (male) rationality and (female) irrationality gives Gilligan's work an additional resonance. This is so because challenges to the narrow definition of morality as concerned with the public world are simultaneously challenges to the exclusive search for a morality of rationality.

Gilligan initiated her studies of women and moral development in part because of her conviction that well-accepted models of morality were androcentric—based upon observation and study of men and reflecting the life patterns and concerns more typical of men than women. The outcomes of her research led her to conclude that there is a moral perspective, typical of women, that does not sacrifice intimacy and the knowledge gained through interpersonal experience to transcendent ideals and the impersonal imperatives of reason. This mode of moral judgment and response she named the perspective of care or responsibility.

Gilligan's work indicts the intentional exclusion of the intimate, particularistic, and emotional from Kohlberg's normative vision of morality. One purpose of her research is to claim that women speak with a moral voice that has been denied both in theory and in practice; moral judgment is less a function of the triumph of pure reason than emotionally pervaded participation in dramas of human relationships. The ethic of care is not bound by the "cognitive constraints" of the justice perspective.[9] Yet Gilligan's own account of the relative roles of reason and emotion in constituting moral response is ambiguous.

Gilligan claims that she will, in her alternative account of moral development, "highlight a distinction between two modes of thought."[10] References to the narratives from which Gilligan builds her theory clarify that she understands it as a theory about "thinking" and "judgment," and as an alternative to other theories about the ways in which people reason about moral dilemmas. "Research on moral judgment has shown that when the categories of women's thinking are examined in detail the outline of a moral conception different from that described by Freud, Piaget or Kohlberg begins to emerge."[11]

Gilligan elucidates a theory of moral reasoning at the same time that she argues against a dichotomizing of reason and emotion. In response to criticisms she writes, for example, that her

critics equate care with feelings, which they oppose to thought, and imagine caring as passive or confined to some separate sphere. I describe care and justice as two moral perspectives that organize both thinking and feelings and empower the self to take different kinds of action in public as well as private life.[12]

"Moral reasoning" and "moral emotions" are inextricable from each other and are mobilized in the context of moral decision-making and action.[13] Gilligan does not claim that the interpretation of the care perspective as related to women's emotional lives is inaccurate, but rather that the dichotomizing of thinking and feeling deforms the meaning of the perspective and lends itself to a polarized definition of gender roles and spheres of activity. In this she is certainly correct.

What, then, is the place of the emotions in moral life? In an essay entitled "The Conquistador and the Dark Continent: Reflections on the Psychology of Love," Gilligan claims that her "interest in conflicting stories about love grew out of [her] research on moral development."[14] Love, she points out, has been denigrated or forgotten as a "central concept in morals."[15] She finds, in fact, that to listen to women talk about moral context and action is to discover that "in talking about morality [women] were in fact talking about love."[16] As a further illustration of the integration, Gilligan resolves the issue of thinking versus feeling as a both/and—not an either/or—phenomenon. She claims that her "portrayal of care reveals its cognitive as well as affective dimensions, its foundation in the ability to perceive people in their own terms and to respond to need."[17]

Such claims toward integration of thought and feeling notwithstanding, a number of commentators on Gilligan's theory have identified a problematic dichotomy. John Broughton, reconstituting Gilligan's position as more extreme than it in fact is, argues that she splits "reason from emotion" and thus is guilty of the "dualism" associated with other psychological models.[18] Iris Marion Young suggests that Gilligan's theoretical subtext challenges a more explicit claim that the theory describes an alternative mode of cognitive functioning. Here it appears that Young is unaware of Gilligan's contrary claims to have discovered a mode of moral response that integrates the "reason and affectivity" with which Young is concerned.[19] But Young's insight remains trenchant; Gilligan does seem to want to define her theory in both ways.

The challenge of theoretically integrating the strands of reason and emotion in Gilligan's theory has been taken up by a political theorist concerned with articulating accounts of the self that oppose the dominant ones of Western political and moral philosophy. Seyla Benhabib opposes a "Kohlbergian" account of the self as the "generalized other"— consistent with and reflective of hegemonic versions of the self and its concerns in this philosophy—and a "Gilliganian," "concrete other." In Benhabib's philosophical reconstruction of Gilligan's moral vision, "moral categories" of "responsibility, bonding and sharing" define the chosen principles that define the norms of action within interactions; accompanying "moral feelings" of "love, care and sympathy, and solidarity" complete the symmetry of response to the other.[20] One problem with this integration, however, is that from Benhabib's own perspective Gilligan's theory is prey to the same criticisms with which Benhabib charges Kohlberg: Not only is the "role of affects" ignored in Kohlberg's theory, but also the roles of "resistance, projection, phantasy, and defense mechanisms," all of which are critical to understanding the "*dynamic* between self and social structure" inherent in the construction of the self.[21] That Gilligan's theory also ignores the emotional adjuncts of these processes is ignored by Benhabib.

Gilligan's dilemma in describing and prescribing the place of emotion in moral selfhood is not merely psychological. It has been problematic for feminists to identify and endorse a predominantly female mode of moral "reasoning" without contributing to a ghettoizing of women in the social and political role of "other." The enterprise becomes particularly fraught with the suggestion that women reason through emotional commitment, a claim that many read as proof that the occupation of a separate— nurturant and empathic—sphere for women reflects the reality of women's and men's different capacities, and not merely socially or historically specific circumstances and experiences. As feminist commentators have noted, ambiguities within Gilligan's work suggest just such conclusions to conservative opponents of the contemporary women's movement, who welcome it as proof of ideological verities about women's nature.[22]

There is one defense of Gilligan that is notable for its attempt to sort out the issue of whether she is theorizing about reason or emotion, and what the implications are for her project. Helen Haste defends Gilligan against the criticism, made by Janet Sayers, that her theory of morality fails to accommodate emotional experiences that diverge from the feminine model of "caring." In defending Gilligan, Haste actually succeeds in sharply defining issues that Gilligan has, perhaps deliberately, left vague.

Haste first clarifies the disciplinary perspective from which Gilligan operates. She argues that Gilligan's theoretical and methodological orientation in the field of cognitive-developmental theory leaves her without a way of adequately theorizing emotions; Gilligan cannot be criticized for excluding certain categories of emotions when it is a feature of her paradigm not to permit the theorist to integrate emotions at all. "It is, indeed, a limitation of cognitive-developmental theory that it quite fails to take *affective* aspects of gender conflict into account."[23] But this clarification is only made along the way to vindicating Gilligan's unique use of a cognitive-developmental account of morality.

The target for Haste is the argument that Gilligan accounts only for a certain class of emotions—empathy, care, love—in developing her alternative vision of morality. Haste, again more unequivocally than Gilligan herself, argues that the ethic of care cannot be confused with "feeling caring," that is, it cannot be confused with a "mode of affect." The care perspective is a principle and, thus, a form of "reasoning about moral dilemmas." The criticism, then, that Gilligan does not adequately integrate all emotions is defused by arguing that Gilligan does not integrate *any* emotions.

If Haste were correct in her delineation of the explanatory reach of Gilligan's theory, it would be difficult to understand why Gilligan understands her "stages" of moral development as fully distinct from those in Kohlberg's account of moral development. Kohlberg argues that judgment according to self-chosen principles, albeit principles of justice, which he understands as indispensable to mature moral judgment, define the highest stage of moral development. Nowhere, on the other hand, does Gilligan speak of the choice of caring as an ethical principle in such a way as to imply that she means the same thing by "principle" as does Kohlberg. This is not, of course, to argue that Gilligan's sparing use of the language of universality and ethical principle signals necessarily the abandonment of concepts associated with these words. It does, however, strongly imply that Gilligan intends to point in quite another direction with her rejection of Kohlberg's developmental theory.

In supporting Gilligan Haste does try, in spite of her explanation of cognitive-developmentalism, not to foreclose the possibility that emotional response constitutes part of the alternative mode of moral judgment that Gilligan wishes to espouse. She suggests that while "the affective state of caring is a legitimate and important part of the moral response, it is not an appeal to feeling *rather than* thinking that is implied."[24] Here Haste sounds more like Gilligan, appealing to the possibility of integrating, rather than dichotomizing, reason and emotion. But this is not the thrust of Haste's argument, as she works to segregate "an *ethic* of care and responsibility" from the "affective response" with which such an ethic bears a linguistic resemblance.[25] The defense of Gilligan's theory offered by Haste underscores the equivocation in Gilligan on the subject of the status of emotions in constituting moral identity. Here, there is much that Gilligan does not clarify. If Kohlberg and others make the mistake of too radically dichotomizing faculties of thinking and feeling, Gilligan resists this temptation. Nevertheless the issue is complicated by the ambiguity of Gilligan's conclusion that the moral perspectives discovered by Kohlberg and herself disclose gendered patterns of response to moral situations.

Thinking, Feeling, and Gender

Gilligan has treated the question of the gendered nature of moral response in a way that is often confusing. Most readers and commentators have understood her landmark (1982) work to make the claim that the different patterns and perspectives identified by herself and Kohlberg are, respectively, female and male patterns and perspectives:

> From a male perspective, a morality of responsibility appears inconclusive and diffuse, given its insistent contextual relativism. Women's moral judgments thus elucidate the pattern observed in the description of the developmental differences observed between the sexes. . . . Given the differences in women's conceptions of self and morality, women bring to the life cycle a different point of view and order human experiences in terms of different priorities.[26]

Gilligan has been reluctant to defend systematically her insights about gender dimorphism in moral response. Indeed, she obfuscates her own strong claims about the gender-boundedness of moral perspective. She often prefers to argue that empirically the care perspective predominates in women's narratives and the justice perspective in men's, this although both women and men can and do show evidence of speaking in a voice not generally associated with members of their sex. "Both voices are—at least in principle—accessible to women and to men."[27] Her work, Gilligan argues, "focuses on the difference between two moral orientations—a justice and a care perspective," not on the issue of differences between women and men per se.[28]

Some of Gilligan's clarification of the issue of gender differences in her theory has been stimulated by critiques. Among the most important of these are: the claim that the gender differences on Kohlberg's moral judgment scale cannot be replicated;[29] the claim that differences found by Gilligan are a function of education,[30] or race and class.[31] The claim that Gilligan underestimates the extent to which the care perspective reproduces the residues of women's socialization to powerlessness is now familiar among students of Gilligan's work.[32]

If Gilligan merely asserts by way of her empirical studies that women are more capable of empathy and emotional responsiveness to the needs of others than men, she is vulnerable to arguments that contest claims of female essentialism.[33] These claims have been linked by feminists to institutionalized forms of oppression and to the truncation of rights and economic and political opportunities for women. Gilligan clearly wishes, on the other hand, to validate experiences of difference apprehended by women who have difficulty situating and recognizing themselves within a social discourse that simultaneously denies and disparages their identities.

The tightrope that Gilligan walks between acknowledging the role of emotion in constituting moral selfhood and speaking of an alternative (female) model of reasoning reflects this dilemma. She cannot assign thinking and feeling to, respectively, men and women; she cannot argue, given her female subjects' self-reports, that emotional responses are outside the sphere of moral thought and action. In respecting her subjects' narratives and weaving them into a coherent theory of moral life, Gilligan seems to be placed in the position of soliciting social recognition and respect for an alternative female "voice" that resounds suspiciously like that of the "angel in the house." To the extent that emotions have a place in moral life they are related to care and responsiveness toward self and proximate others and remain the special domain of women.

Gilligan amply demonstrates that she does not wish to construct a moral theory that dichotomizes reason and emotion within the moral self, although she points to an empirical separation between gendered selves. Part of her project is to confront hegemonic moral theories with a theory that integrates thinking and feeling. Her narrative accounts of moral dilemmas are cast as taking place in the context of caring relations with others. Yet, as Gilligan acknowledges, relatedness to others often does not occur in such a context of care; moreover, the feelings that help to construct relatedness partake of a broader range of human emotions than those presented by Gilligan's theory. It is the disagreeable emotions that remain to be introduced into the ethic of care and the description of relations.

The Problem of Aggression

Two feminist theorists from different disciplines have criticized Gilligan's theory based upon her account of emotion. Both N. Katherine Hayles and Janet Sayers understand Gilligan to make the claim that her model of moral development represents an attempt to integrate emotional response into a general account of moral life; both criticize what they understand as an exclusion of consideration of emotions of hatred and anger from Gilligan's theory.

Many respondents to Gilligan have by this time pointed out implications of the fact that the evidence that supports her theory is in the form of solicited self-reports. Zella Luria points out that Gilligan does not have "a sound basis for talking about peoples' behavior, only for analyzing what they say."[34] Similarly, Annette C. Baier notes that Gilligan studies not emotions but "intellectual reflections."[35] The use of subjects' narratives as the basis for a theory like Gilligan's has been questioned by a number of critics. The most strenuous objections have come from John M. Broughton, who argues that the fact that subjects are taken at their word risks self-deception; in Gilligan's theory, "self and self-concept are assumed to be identical."[36]

There is, however, another perspective that takes Gilligan's work as itself constituting a narrative, with the theorist as architect of the narrative. From this perspective, Broughton suggests that Gilligan selectively presents and interprets her subjects' responses, and that this shaping of the research material enhances her thesis.[37] Whatever the validity of this particular claim, a related argument, offered by a feminist literary critic, provides additional insight into the anger that is missing from Gilligan's theory.

N. Katherine Hayles begins her comparison of the perspective of care in Gilligan's theoretical text and George Eliot's *Mill on the Floss* by arguing that the genre categories that they occupy are not entirely distinct; both are texts that tell a story through a narrator's "voice." Gilligan writes "not about life but about narratives" and constructs a text that is itself a narrative—one that is "shaped by and inextricable from the voice that tells the story." What does this voice do? Hayles argues that Gilligan's narrative voice not only tells the story of an ethic of care but also participates in "suppress[ing] the sound of women's anger."[38]

Through an analysis of Gilligan's rhetorical and interpretive styles, Hayles traces a narrative strategy that she sees culminating in a denial of women's feelings of anger and hatred. Returning to Gilligan's text, Hayles examines Gilligan's subjects' responses and Gilligan's interpretive framework itself for clues about Gilligan's transformation of the expression of emotion into theory. As Hayles finds in Gilligan's text a transmuting of "hating" (in the story of Jenny) into "tension" and women's sense of being "suspended between an ideal of selflessness and the truth of their own agency and needs,"[39] she similarly finds in Gilligan an inadequate reading of Eliot's text that expunges from it the centrality of anger: "Gilligan's narrative illustrates . . . the ways in which anger is repressed or not expressed because it conflicts with the assumption of an ethic of care."[40]

The anger of which Hayles writes is passion with a specifiable cause and object: institutionalized and coercively enforced masculine authority over women, and the denial of women's selfhood. In her criticisms of Gilligan, Sayers also conceptualizes anger in this fashion. Sayers addresses the moral perspective of care directly, comparing a "Freudian" account of gender and moral development with the cognitive-developmental work of Kohlberg and Gilligan. Her argument is that Gilligan's method cannot adequately capture—and thus examine the roots and significance of—women's "contrary intentions": caring and noncaring, loving and hating. Citing the analytic case of one of Freud's female patients, Sayers concludes that "although women are indeed concerned with caring as Gilligan claims, they also have contrary intentions—intentions that may, on account of this contradiction, be unconscious and not immediately manifest, especially to the types of investigation used by Gilligan."[41]

Gilligan addresses Sayers's criticisms directly, arguing that she does uncover in her narrative the contrary (to care) intentions expressed by her subjects.[42] Gilligan adduces the response of Sarah from her text to support her contention that anger and hatred are neither expunged by her nor suppressed by her subjects themselves. Yet the narrative strategies by which Hayles argues that Gilligan transforms these emotions is in evidence in Gilligan's proffered case. Sarah states that she is "pretty frustrated and a lot angrier than I admit, a lot more aggressive than I admit"; her dilemma is understood by Gilligan to involve the integration of "directness" and "self-assertion" into her relationships. Anger is coextensive with directness; aggression is equated with self-assertion.[43]

Gilligan argues that Sayers "negate[s] from the outset the possibility of a different voice, that is, a voice that recasts the terms of psychological discourse to include both the experiences of women and a different way of thinking about the self, morality, and human development."[44] Yet Gilligan misapprehends the criticism that both Sayers and Hayles can arguably be understood as addressing, albeit from quite different perspectives. If Gilligan is understood as contributing more to discourse about morality than her claims about gender differences in reasoning about moral issues—if she is understood as theorizing the terms of a relational morality that takes seriously the role of emotional process and development in constituting morality—then the arguments of these particular critics challenge Gilligan (and others) to consider what might be missing from her account of emotions and relations.[45] They do not argue that Gilligan misunderstands the nature of morality and human relations altogether; they suggest directions in which a theory like Gilligan's might progress.

In at least two of Gilligan's works she has written of what she calls "the problem of aggression," in *In a Different Voice* claiming it as a problem that "both sexes face."[46] In "Images of Violence,"[47] the authors note but do not endorse the suggestion that women deal with aggression differently than men—hence, deviantly—by disclaiming it and transforming it into something unrecognizable. In this particular essay "aggression" is defined as "the intent of one individual to hurt another."[48] At other times it is not as clear what Gilligan means by aggression, aside from its obvious aspect: physical violence, which, as she points out, is far more often practiced by men than by women.

As regards women, Gilligan fails to integrate in a thorough fashion the insights that she does raise about the nature of aggression—hatred, anger, and their effects—with one exception: the argument that women and men project violent imagery into, respectively, scenes of isolation and achievement (women) and intimacy (men).[49] Thus, though Gilligan attends throughout her work to the emotional implications of relationships, especially for women, her central argument about rage and aggression suggests that women experience these feelings primarily (if not only) when the possibility of relationship is denied. Kate, one of Gilligan's adolescent subjects, reports:

I called my mother up and said, "Why can't I speak to you anymore? What is going on?" And I ended up crying and hanging up on her because she wouldn't listen to me. . . . And you know, I kept saying, "Well, you hurt me," and she said, "No, I did not." And I said, "Well, why am I hurt?" you know, and she is just denying my feelings as if they did not exist and as if I had no right to feel them, you know, even though they were.[50]

In commenting on Kate, Gilligan does not deny the anguish and anger communicated by the words. But her interpretation of Kate's dilemma opposes connection, or "genuine connection" as Gilligan says here, to the anger and bitterness experienced by the mother and daughter. She does not dwell on the possibility that people, including women, can be bound to one another in relationships of love that are simultaneously relationships of anger and disappointment.

In her early book Gilligan quotes Sophie Tolstoy, the wife of Leo Tolstoy, and cites her as an example of a woman who, confronting the pain of her relationship with her husband, chooses to try not to love. Gilligan gives Tolstoy as an example of a woman in a state of "moral nihilism," as one of many women who attempt to "cut off their feelings and not care."[51] Gilligan's equation of "love" with "feeling" in her interpretation of Tolstoy's dilemma is consistent with her theory. The experience of emotions other than empathy and love are defined a priori as antithetical to relationship, as destructive to connection. Gilligan's "alternative vision of the web of connection" constructs a "recognition of relationship that prevents aggression and gives rise to the understanding that generates response."[52] Yet as long as disagreeable passions are construed as outside the boundaries of legitimate and desirable forms of relationship, a theory of care cannot conceptualize the full range of human response and connection. In making care (or love) synonymous with emotion, and in defining away the significance of anger and hatred, Gilligan gives us particular and embodied selves. But these selves remain one-dimensional. This stark distinction between love and connection (on the one hand) and disconnection (on the other) is the foundation of Gilligan's rejection of a psychoanalytic account of women's moral identity.

Gilligan's Rejection of Psychoanalytic Theory

In the introductory chapter of *In a Different Voice*, Gilligan addresses the theoretical strategies of two psychoanalytic predecessors on the issue of gender differences. First she notes Freud's famous analysis of the role of the superego in constituting the foundations of morality, including Freud's denunciation of women's moral impulses, "influenced" as they are "by feelings of affection and hostility."[53] Next, Gilligan identifies the misogynistic subtext of Erik Erikson's account of mature identity formation. Women's identities are constituted in the course of relationships and are inextricable from them; men's identities are constructed prior to embarking on mature forms of intimacy. Masculine identity and mature identity are synonymous.

The theme that Gilligan reads in both of the psychoanalytic arguments that she briefly surveys is that of separation: the masculine preoccupation with "separation, autonomy, individuation and natural rights" that has been transformed into a "developmental litany."[54] In Freud, the emphasis on the developmental urgency of the boy's separation from mother and from instinctual satisfaction that initiates the formation of superego is also an emphasis on aggression. The superego directs against the ego not only the internalized aggression of the external authority (the father) but also—and more importantly—the instinctual aggression that must not be turned outward against others and the aggression generated by the frustration of having to renounce erotic pleasures in the service of resolving the Oedipus complex.[55] For Freud, the processes of separation and moral development are funded with aggression.

Gilligan does not argue at length about the shortcomings of a psychoanalytic perspective on moral theory. She suggests, as many feminists have, that traditional psychoanalytic theory is misogynist in its assumptions, its methods, and its normative prescriptions. In dismissing the gender-differential theories of Freud and Erikson, Gilligan dismisses theories of gender and moral life that are biased toward a concern with issues of separation rather than attachment. The psychoanalytic theorists she examines both represent this bias; the inclusion of the critique provides a vehicle for Gilligan to suggest that psychoanalytic theory cannot illuminate the issues peculiar to women's moral identity.

The position that Gilligan takes toward an orthodox, "Freudian" psychoanalytic theory is similar to that which she adopts toward object relations thought. Gilligan deplores Nancy Chodorow's dependence on object relations theory, suggesting that object relations "ties the formation of the self to the experience of separation, joining separation with individuation and thus counterposing the experience of the self to the experience of connection with others."[56] It is not just an instinct/drive account of human nature that Gilligan wishes to oppose; all psychoanalytic theory suffers from the problem of understanding human development in terms of male development, in which the primary developmental issues revolve around separation, individuation, and the maintenance of autonomy. No psychoanalytic perspective, it seems, can encompass the themes from which she constructs her vision of women's morality. This even though Gilligan acknowledges that "separation and attachment" constitute a "dialectic" that is woven inextricably into human development and moral life.[57]

There is little in Gilligan's writings on the relevance of psychoanalytic theory for the study of morality. Likewise, there is no systematic effort to examine the various orientations, models, and perspectives within the broad designation of "psychoanalysis" to determine whether any of these might survive the rejection of psychoanalytic theory implied by her rejection of orthodox Freudian theory. This is not necessarily a criticism of Gilligan; it is not part of her project to survey the literature of the various psychologies for a complete account of their treatment of themes related to the study of moral life. However, Gilligan makes a claim to have distinguished in women a "different voice," a style of moral response previously unheard by psychologists and philosophers. This claim can be interrogated.

Klein and the Morality of Reparation

As the philosopher Bernard Williams points out, Kleinian theory provides a way of linking the emotions (such as guilt, compassion, and the like) with responsiveness and action in situations of moral choice.[58] This link is the Kleinian account of reparation. Klein's first references to an inchoate notion of reparation appeared early in her career, in 1929. At that time she was less concerned with the maturation of moral capacities than with the defensive uses and consequences of anxiety. Elaboration of the "depressive position" to which the notion of reparation would ultimately be related came in a 1935 paper. It was, finally, with the publication in 1937 of her essay "Love, Guilt and Reparation" that Klein extended and clarified her ideas about the centrality of care and reparation in psychic life.

With her account of morality in the "depressive position," Klein separated herself theoretically from the formulations of Freud and his followers on the nature of moral life; although she continued to employ the Freudian language of superego and Oedipus, her usage undermines the easy accommodation of such terms to Freudian theory. To Freud's construction of human moral life as a tapestry of rage, aggression, renunciation, loss, and interpersonal fragility, Klein added the possibility of love and commitment. But this was more than a mere addition to orthodox (Freudian) psychoanalytic thought.

According to Eli Sagan, Freud himself conceptualized "the history of the world" as "a fateful struggle between love and hatred."[59] Sagan predicates his argument about the possibility of loving and morally good societies on Freudian foundations: eros, identification, the sublimation of aggression. Yet Sagan's easy identity of love and Freudian eros is problematic. As C. Fred Alford points out, eros (and this includes Freudian eros) is fundamentally greedy and selfish, wishing to draw from the world, hence from others, the goodness that sates desire and need. Love, conversely, must recognize the independent reality and integrity of the object and be capable of sacrifice on the other's behalf.[60] Eros alone cannot furnish the foundations of a morality based on love of, or concern for, others.

Thus, Gilligan and other feminists are correct in their assessment that Freudian psychoanalysis is unable to offer a theoretical foundation for a morality of care. In fact it is Klein, rather than Freud, who is able to illuminate a morality of love and, more generally, a morality of the passions. The significance of Klein's turn from Freud is revealed in part by Klein's notion of "positions," and by the moral values and relational capacities consistent with each of the positions that she delineates.

Positions in Klein's theory are not developmental stages, in the sense, for example, of oral, anal, and genital stages which, once reached, represent an irreversible developmental achievement. "Position" refers instead to a complex constellation of perceptions, phantasies, emotions, and behaviors, some of which serve as defenses against forms of anxiety that are either "paranoid-schizoid" or "depressive" in origin. Meltzer points out that as Klein's thinking about the content of each position evolved over her career, so also did her thinking about the concept "position" itself. Klein's later thought on the positions was that they are "manifestations of crucial attitudes towards the [internal and external] objects," that is to say, intrinsically related to moral feelings and inter-pretation concerning the self and others.[61] "Positions become areas of object-relations in which different value systems prevail."[62]

In the "earlier," paranoid-schizoid phase of development the infant (self), under the necessity of fear of disintegration, splits its inchoate loving and hating feelings and rigidly segregates them. Neither the self nor others can be perceived or experienced realistically under the conditions of such a radical splitting; no relation with others of care or love is conceivable.[63] It is not until a successful integration of these feelings begins to occur that a morality of care becomes a possibility. This integration signals the onset of what Klein called the depressive po-sition.

Hanna Segal, a close collaborator of Klein's, defines the depressive position as "that phase of development in which the infant recognizes a whole object and relates himself to that object."[64] The position is ushered in by the realization, assisted by maturing cognitive powers, that the world (internal and external) that had been divided into "good" and "bad" is not, in fact, divided along these lines. The realization is often expressed in this way: "Good mother" and "bad mother" are the same mother.

An increasingly sophisticated perception of others entails the—often painful and frightening—integration of loving and hating feelings toward them. The child fears the vehemence not only of its hate but also of its love; it fears that these emotions are powerful enough to destroy significant external others, as well as the internal images of "goodness" on which relations with the self and others depend. The child fears as well that it will not be sufficiently powerful to protect the objects of its concern, hence Klein's understanding of the child's "depression" in the face of what seems an unmanageable task. As R. D. Hinshelwood points out, it is primarily to protect the goodness and nurturance of our own internal world that we begin the "depressive" practice of reparation, exercising care through phantasies and actions. But it would be inaccurate to characterize Klein's account of reparation as solipsistic.

> Making reparation—which is such an essential part of the ability to love—widens in scope, and the child's capacity to accept love and, by various means, to take into [herself or] himself goodness from the outer world steadily increases. . . . The essential capacity for "give and take" has been developed in us in a way that ensures our own contentment, and contributes to the pleasure, comfort or happiness of other people.[65]

Reparative activities lay the necessary foundation for mutual and empathic relations with others and are a natural occurrence in healthy development. Such activities are, as Segal underscores, directed to the real mother and later toward real others; they are not merely phantasized preoccupations of an intrapsychically directed self, as some of Klein's critics would maintain. Throughout life depressive anxiety remains: the unconscious fear that one's efforts will not suffice to protect and nurture. For Klein, "depressive anxiety is never fully overcome . . . the fate of one's objects in the face of one's own conflictual feelings remains a central concern throughout life."[66]

Klein, Winnicott, and the Disagreeable Passions

Donald Winnicott did adopt, albeit with reservations and modifications, Melanie Klein's concept of the depressive position. He shifted the focus of theoretical interest further than Klein away from the internal dynamics of the developing self, drawing attention to the nature of "maternal preoccupation": the quality of actual response to the emotional needs of the child. He criticized Klein's ostensibly rigorous and judgmental normative standard of mental/moral health. He vacillated on the fruitfulness and descriptiveness of the very concept of "positions," preferring to speak more fluidly of "capacities." He remained unreconciled to the language, if not the implications, of Klein's concept of reparation when he wrote of a "stage of concern." However, in spite of these differences, Winnicott's account of the central role played by the disagreeable passions in development is more like Klein's than is sometimes assumed.

The crudest version of the origin of hatred, anger, and aggression in Klein's theory would have these passions issuing from the workings of the death instinct and from frustrations associated with denials of drive satisfaction. Believing that this account collapsed too wide a variety of emotions and developmental moves into too few categories, Winnicott strove for a more precise taxonomy.

Winnicott argues that the earliest expressions of what Klein calls hatred are actually "primitive love." "Mature" hatred requires integrative and developmental powers of which the infant is not yet capable; it requires perception of the complete other. What the infant can do is direct a demanding, ruthless, seemingly annihilating "love" at its (incompletely perceived) care giver.[67] This care-less use of the mother by the infant does arouse, so Winnicott argues, the mature hatred of the mother. If the mother resists the urge to retaliate, the likelihood of healthy development on the part of the child, including the recognition of its own mature aggressiveness, is increased. It is necessary, Winnicott argues, that the child experience both the hating and loving feelings of the care giver. It is in this way that the child comes to feel "real"; that is, that all aspects of its self have been experienced and acknowledged.[68]

Early primitive love is eventually superseded by a mature capacity for both love and hatred. In Winnicott's version of the "depressive position," his "stage of concern," aspects of primitive love impulses begin to be recognized by the child as potentially harmful to the others who are simultaneously coming into existence as objects of mature love and concern. Winnicott's and Klein's accounts of anger and hatred are little distinct on this score: the negotiation of feelings of rage and hatred is an indispensable task of development and will remain so throughout life.

In spite of Winnicott's noted propensity to explain development in social or "environmental" terms, he does understand mature rage and hatred as in large measure a function of the *necessary* frustration of instinctual desires. Under these conditions maturity will eventually demand "an acceptance of responsibility for all the destructiveness that is bound up with living, with the instinctual life, and with anger at frustration."[69] For both Klein and Winnicott the mere project of living entails frustrations so prodigious that disagreeable passions are created and must be managed.

In Klein's (and Winnicott's) account of moral life, the healthy and— a not inconsiderable conclusion—interpersonally desirable solution is in the human capacity for reparation. Both theorists point out that human beings are reluctant to acknowledge the disagreeable emotions in themselves; both argue that genuine love and reparative concern require such acknowledgment. "The human individual cannot accept the destructive and aggressive ideas in his or her own nature without experience of reparation."[70] At the same time, "constructive effort is false and meaningless unless . . . one has first reached to the destruction."[71]

Reparation and Care

Carol Gilligan has produced a comprehensive and provocative vision of (especially women's) moral life. In it she identifies both empirically and normatively a model of moral identity and response; this model demonstrates the centrality of emotional processes and experience to moral reasoning and action. Gilligan argues that this rendition of moral development is unique, and indeed, for the most part, it is. But Gilligan's rejection of psychoanalytic theory is too hasty to take account of possible predecessors.

In Melanie Klein's (object relational) moral theory neither masculine development nor the desired outcomes of separation and detachment are privileged. Instead, the maintenance of relationships is consistently given as a goal. As Donald Winnicott points out, Klein brings to psychoanalysis a way of conceptualizing not only individual psychic "health" but also the more perplexing dimension of human "value."[72] Klein proposes a model of moral life that is sensitive to the centrality of loving, empathic care for others. Reparation is, of necessity, an *interpersonal* process; it, like the experience of emotion itself, presupposes the existence and meaningfulness of others whose fates are of concern.

Gilligan's theory of moral life and a Kleinian account have in common an insistence upon empathy, care, and love as foundations of a certain kind of (neglected) understanding and practice of morality. Although both the similarities and differences have not been thoroughly explored critically, at least one psychoanalyst has noted a possible comity between the theories.[73] Yet, in spite of important similarities between the two, differences remain.

A number of Gilligan's critics have noted the possibility that her theory has in some measure incorporated (perhaps unconscious) evasions as unproblematic self-assessments. A Kleinian moral theory, because of its derivation from "deep" analysis of subjects, is less prey to this criticism. Klein suggests that the disagreeable passions, by far less evident in the reports of Gilligan's subjects, are foundational in the formation of self and relational capacities. Klein also argues that it is these passions that are most frequently denied, being perceived as dangerous both to the self and others.

Gilligan has argued, in response to critics, that hatred, rage, and other disagreeable passions are not missing from her account. Yet anger and hatred, when they are included, are assimilated only sporadically; their inclusion appears less intrinsic than incidental to Gilligan's account of morality. Instead of hatred and rage, and the fear of these emotions, Gilligan mentions "moral outrage" and "moral passion" as results of the failure or loss of "human connection."[74] These passions vanish when the situations that give rise to them are amended.

In Kleinian moral theory the capacity to make reparation is not only a developmental achievement but also "a fundamental element in love and in all human relationships."[75] The emotional integration demanded by this capacity is, she argues, constantly being performed. Reparation implies the necessity to repair, to reconstitute, to, in Klein's words, "make good" that which has been threatened or endangered. When Gilligan writes of a "restorative activity of care" and of reparation her language does not imply the experience of anger or destructive desire that informs Klein's perspective. This is true even when she argues that women seek to undo harms that have been done either to themselves or others. Ambivalence toward the other does not play a part in precipitating the moral obligation to "provide help" and take "responsibility for one another."[76]

In spite of a transformative view of the connections between morality and emotional experience, Gilligan's theory is flawed by inattention to a certain class of emotions: the disagreeable emotions of anger and hatred. Gilligan's misattribution to psychoanalytic theory of an *exclusive* concern with insular individuality underscores her conviction that that body of theory cannot be useful in conceptualizing the relational emotional processes and their role in moral response. Her error helps to obscure the relevance of a psychodynamic object relations perspective to an ethic of care.

Conclusion

In grounding the abstract self of Kohlberg's psychology and communitarian politics in the lived reality of relationships, Gilligan has transformed the nature of much social theorizing. In the years since Gilligan first began to develop her vision, her work has been subject to an astounding variety of critiques in numerous academic disciplines. The very range of interest testifies to the ways in which she has stimulated dialogue and reformulation of orthodoxies. Her challenge to psychology has infiltrated a vast range of disciplines and assisted a contemporary revolution in ways of understanding the nature of selfhood.

Even so, Gilligan has successfully explained only one aspect of the hold of relations with others on the self, and that aspect that we are most likely to want to acknowledge about ourselves. The remaining aspects of relations and of the self are quietly pushed back—to the margins of consciousness and social theory. In the end, the absence of a depth psychology limits Gilligan to asserting that relations are foundational to human being but leaves her unable to explain why this is so.

A Kleinian moral theory can provide a way to correct this omission. By acknowledging the ubiquity and functions of the disagreeable passions, Kleinian theory accomplishes much: it does not deny gender differences but instead challenges the theorist to locate differences in the context of the human struggle with the passions; it restores the denied parts of the narrative of feeling to moral and social theory. Far from being identical to the orthodox psychoanalytic theories that Gilligan rejects, Klein takes up the challenge of understanding the dialectic of the formation of selves within social context. This challenge is one that Gilligan has already embraced in articulating and defending her moral vision.

Gilligan is critical of feminist applications of psychoanalytic theory. Nonetheless, the work of Nancy Chodorow and Jessica Benjamin can be understood as continuous with Gilligan's project of representing the self as relational. These projects diverge not, as Gilligan would have it, because the psychoanalytic method is flawed but because Chodorow and Benjamin more successfully penetrate familiar self-conceptions and cherished social arrangements. They illuminate more, and more problematic, aspects of the self than Gilligan can accommodate.

CHAPTER 4

The Passions in Feminist Object Relations

From the black pines you have borrowed
this calm autonomy, these callous masks
of ice. From bone fires you shy, from
any extremity, from aftermaths of ash.
December's dusk and snow-sough whisper
bark is beyond loving, beyond loathing,
free of rage or memory or any need.
Too weak for flame, you swallow winter.
      —Jeff Mann,
       "Frost Fugue"

Object Relations Feminism

Nancy Chodorow and Jessica Benjamin have in common their use of object relations theory to analyze individual development, gender inequality, and, more generally, social issues of power and domination. Like Gilligan, Chodorow and Benjamin undermine the communitarian model of selfhood that passes for an alternative to the rationalism and abstract individualism of liberalism. They do this by inquiring into the unconscious character of psychic development and the fluid and complex forms of interaction between self and other. Unlike Gilligan, they do not depend on self-assessments as the basis for theory. Combining clinical experience, psychoanalytic theory, and social theory, their analyses of psychic life penetrate more deeply into the repetition of everyday relations and social conventions. Gilligan does insist, as do the communitarians in different ways, that women confront refractory moral dilemmas as issues of relations. Chodorow and Benjamin shift the focus; theirs is an attempt to build social theory by illuminating aspects of relations beyond conscious awareness.

The work of Nancy Chodorow, Jessica Benjamin, and Dorothy Dinnerstein has helped to shape and direct the course of much modern feminist thought. The following analyses of Chodorow and Benjamin focus narrowly on a particular area: the way in which each theorist responds to the disagreeable passions in her theory of selfhood. Because Chodorow responds less directly to the role of these passions in constituting selfhood, the discussion of her work concentrates upon their absence and its significance. Benjamin speaks to the passions in her account of deformations of the self but disposes of the disagreeable passions nonetheless.

Using the ideas of Klein and Winnicott as a ground of comparison, the strategies by which both Chodorow and Benjamin marginalize the disagreeable passions become apparent. Both Chodorow and Benjamin position their work as consistent with the ideas of Donald Winnicott; neither relates her ideas to Melanie Klein. More significantly, each enacts different developmental mechanisms to deal with the disagreeable passions, and these can be challenged from the perspective of the very object relations theory from which these feminist theories are derived.

Nancy Chodorow: Gender and Mothering

Chodorow's now-famous work calls upon psychoanalytic theory to address issues of gender identity, inequality, and relational life. Feminists have long understood such issues as indispensable to the study of women's social position, and Chodorow's contributions to feminist thought in these areas are prodigious. The analyses for which she is best known include: first, her reconstruction of the gendered nature of early development, especially the vicissitudes of identification with, and separation from, the mother; and, second, her account of the "reproduction of mothering" itself. By this is meant the processes of psychological development that predispose women toward nurturance of children, and thereby help to reproduce the sex/gender system.

The psychoanalytic theory fashioned by Chodorow synthesizes the work of many early object relations theorists, including Michael Balint, W. R. D. Fairbairn, Harry Guntrip, and Donald Winnicott. In her early book, Chodorow classifies Melanie Klein with Freud as a drive theorist, rather than as a theorist of object relations, and rejects the salience of Kleinian theory to her work.[1]

It is significant that the rejection of Kleinian theory is largely predicated on Klein's emphasis on the disagreeable passions. Moreover, it is noteworthy that Chodorow has been most instrumental in introducing what is now most often understood as part of a Kleinian perspective into contemporary feminist theory.[2] Chodorow argues persuasively that in order to understand female development and experience it is necessary to concentrate analysis on the earliest period of life, and on the relations between mothers and children.

Psychological life and interpersonal experience are mutually constitutive in Chodorow's reconstruction of early life. Gendered patterns of selfhood are a result. Female development is structured through identification with mother and the internalizations and sense of self that result. To be more accurate, the female child's sense of self is constructed within a dense network of mutual identifications between mother and daughter. In part due to her own situation of relative powerlessness, and especially as a result of emotional isolation, the mother not only cares for her daughter but also simultaneously identifies with her.

The mother's emotional embrace is the crucible of, among other things, the more flexible ego boundaries that the daughter will carry into adulthood. The consequence is a desire and capacity to affiliate, to experience continuity of self and other:

Girls emerge from this [oedipal] period with a basis for "empathy" built into their primary definition of self in a way that boys do not. Girls emerge with a stronger basis for experiencing another's needs or feelings as one's own (or of thinking that one is so experiencing another's needs and feelings).[3]

Male development is structured through differentiation from mother, in fact, by rejection of identification with her. Instead, in spite of the emotional bond between them, boys "dread" mother. Further, they strive to establish themselves as male by emulating abstract masculine role requirements rather than identifying affectively with fathers and other males, who are usually emotionally, if not physically, absent.[4] The consequence is a process of individuation in males that precludes affiliation as a basic aspect of the "sense of self."

The institution of mothering is both cause and effect of these developmental dynamics. It must be understood that by "mothering" Chodorow means all that is usually understood to be implied by this term, and not just gestating and giving birth. The contrast between what is connoted by "fathering" and what by "mothering" is additional evidence of mothering as a richly constituted sphere of social labor and symbolism. It is the "reproduction of mothering" as a social, economic, political, and ideological construct with which Chodorow is primarily concerned. Thus, her interest is not only in identifying the static situation of women: relegated to a "private" sphere, affectively balancing the rationalistic world outside, socializing children, performing unpaid work. Her interest is in dissecting the relationship between the psychological birth-process in gendered human beings and both the greater capacity and desire for affiliation in women than in men.

What Chodorow delineates is a set of gendered ideal types. Using this schema, she concludes that women are not simply coerced into performing the plethora of emotional, physical, and intellectual tasks associated socially with mothering; neither are they merely socialized to perform them. Women want to mother, Chodorow maintains, and for explicable reasons are uniquely suited to mothering. A personality structure in females that fits the requirements of the nurturant, care-giving female role in turn ensures the perpetuation of females in that role.

Women, as mothers, produce daughters with mothering capacities and the desire to mother. These capacities and needs are built into and grow out of the mother-daughter relationship itself. By contrast, women as mothers (and men as not-mothers) produce sons whose nurturant capacities and needs have been systematically curtailed and repressed. . . . The sexual and familial division of labor in which women mother and are more involved in interpersonal, affective relationships than men produces in daughters and sons a division of psychological capacities which leads them to reproduce this sexual and familial division of labor.[5]

Chodorow is credited by feminist critics of object relations theory with having assumed the perspective of the mother rather than merely presuming the existence of females as a class of available, affectively providing persons.[6] Even so, her theory of mothering and affective development draws upon a tradition of object relations theory that reconstructs emotional life from its origins. This tradition theorizes the existence of passions of rage, anxiety, hatred, and aggression as intrinsic to human connection.

The role of disagreeable passions does not occupy a central place in Chodorow's story of gendered development. Indeed, all the passions are treated equivocally. It is useful to focus on the nature of and reasons for this equivocation; from them it is possible to discern that Chodorow is of two minds about the place of the passions in a feminist account of selfhood.

Mature Relations and the Unreasonable Child

Much of *The Reproduction of Mothering* is given over to a painstaking psychoanalytic reconstruction of the gendered nature of psychic development. In it, Chodorow explains from an object relational perspective the psychological processes that are foundational in the creation of personality and psychic structure: projection, introjection, identification, displacement, splitting. "Unconscious operations" are, she contends, ubiquitous and normal aspects of the construction of an inner world. Further, the internal world is not merely a container or a mirror image of what it takes in from the outside; the processes are "mediated by fantasy and by conflict."[7] In fact, the theorist that emerges from this discussion seems unrelated to the one criticized by Toril Moi, and others, for "not tak[ing] the unconscious sufficiently into account."[8] Chodorow's account here is subtle. It recognizes the constant transactions between inner and outer reality: "A person lives in a multiple object world—in the internal largely unconscious object world of their psyche which has laid its foundations in the past, in childhood, and in the external, largely conscious world of daily life."[9] It is primarily in the application of object relations theory to gender, her account of how the configuration and content of internalizations and defenses vary between women and men, that Chodorow's object relations is an innovation.

On the other hand, however, is yet another Chodorow, one who excoriates fantasy and feeling (especially about or directed toward "mother") and urges their replacement by a realistic perception of others. In essays such as "The Fantasy of the Perfect Mother"[10] and

"Feminism and Difference," among others, Chodorow either ignores the psychic processes that object relations thinkers find constitutive of internal life, or she writes as though they are superfluous to—or subversive of—healthy development.[11] In the earlier of the essays, Chodorow and Contratto go so far as to indict "post-Freudian psychological theory" for much of the "popular view that the relationship of mother and infant has extraordinary significance."[12] This uncompromising statement is startling in light of Chodorow's own position as a prominent post-Freudian theorist, and especially one who has eloquently defended psychoanalytic object relations theory from the attacks of other feminists. Can these apparent contradictions be reconciled? The answer is that they can, once the theme that connects much of Chodorow's work is clarified.

In many of her essays, Chodorow is concerned with articulating possible solutions to the problem of relations between the self and others. In one, for example, she suggests a "relational individualism" consistent with the tenets of object relations theory.[13] However, the failure to recognize and value the independent subjectivity of women, a failure that has been a pervasive and usually invisible fact of intimate and social relations, complicates this problem.[14] Chodorow appears to solve this problem by decrying and rejecting fantasy and the passions—those attributes of humanness without which a more objective receptivity toward the outer world might be possible.

This is, of course, to simplify the arguments in Chodorow's various works. But considering the problem, and her solution, in this way helps to make sense of many of the conflicts contained, often uneasily, in those works. It means that when Chodorow turns from constructing explanatory arguments about earliest developmental processes to appraising normative solutions her most penetrating analyses of psychological processes and the passions are abandoned.

In these normative arguments, "the child" is seen to be possessed of "unreasonable" and "unrealistic" needs, demands, and (it is easy to infer from the argument) feelings and desires.[15] These the mother, as a real human being with a separate existence, cannot legitimately be expected to satisfy. This is admittedly an extreme example of Chodorow's hostility to the illogic of internal life. But other illustrations can be drawn from an essay that is arguably one of her finest: her critique of Herbert Marcuse and Norman O. Brown in "Beyond Drive Theory: Object Relations and the Limits of Radical Individualism."[16]

Chodorow's target in this piece is a pair of individualistic, infant-pleasure-oriented utopian social theories. Marcuse[17] and Brown[18] take the perspective of the child and transform it into a total emotional/sexual/social/political vision. Chodorow responds by assuming the perspective of women/mothers, which is simultaneously the perspective of the adult. She upholds the necessity of recognizing the subjectivity of others, especially women, and supports mature relational life. The vehicle for this perspective is an incisive demonstration of the dependence of theories of libidinal liberation on the use of women, and the denial of subjectivity to women.

In order to make this kind of argument, Chodorow rejects the passions (and the drives, especially in "Beyond Drive Theory"). The passions are disclaimed because this strategy is perceived to be the only way to ensure against the solipsistic anticommunity of Marcuse and Brown. More generally, it is Chodorow's response to the assumption underlying visions of community throughout the history of political thought, including communitarianism, of the availability of women's nurturance of men and children.

Thus, Chodorow does not merely denounce the disagreeable passions nor deny their pertinence to women's development. She abandons all the passions instead and embroils herself in contradiction. Significantly, Chodorow's objection to Dinnerstein underscores the position of the disagreeable emotions in the work of each. Chodorow and Contratto point out that Dinnerstein's "recommendation for shared parenting stems from her wish that the inevitable rage toward caretakers be shared between women and men."[19] This is indeed what Dinnerstein suggests; Chodorow's suggestion seems instead to be the substitution of "intersubjectivity" and "mature dependence" for "rage" and other passions.[20]

However sensitive her account of early gender development, the truncation of the disagreeable passions, their failure to survive the demands of mature relation, leaves her open to criticism, even—and perhaps especially—from object relations theory. Chodorow is consistent in her rejection of Klein, in her disavowal of Klein as an object relations theorist. The form of such rejections is significant. Chodorow argues, for example, that Klein overestimated aggressiveness because aggressive behavior is so much more obvious that tranquil behavior in infants.[21] Here Chodorow appears forgetful at best; she has already maintained in the same work that psychoanalytic theory does not assume a "one-to-one correspondence" between affect and behavior.[22] The portrayal of Klein as a theorist of the drives and aggression, followed by a rejection of her, is revelatory. A reevaluation of aspects of Klein's thought provides tools for criticizing the absence of the disagreeable passions in Chodorow.

Melanie Klein: The Balance of Love and Hate

A critique of Chodorow's theory from the perspective of integrating the disagreeable passions could proceed, given the breadth of Chodorow's work, in a number of ways. This is so because what is most at issue is not what she does say about these passions, but rather what is omitted. However, a fruitful point of reference for such a critique is available in her germinal work. This is the way that Chodorow locates and theorizes "ambivalence" in the original relation between child and caretaker.

The Reproduction of Mothering is rife with references to ambivalence, both in the first relation (usually with mother or another woman) and later relations. Chodorow concurs with much psychoanalytic theory that every individual enters life with "innate erotic and aggressive energies." These energies are not, she hastens to add, "drives" seeking satisfaction, in the Freudian sense, but energies that become quickly transfigured by the human search for relationship. What is puzzling is that there is a substantial place in Chodorow's vision of development, relations, and maturity for impulses that bear some relation to the "erotic" energies of which she speaks, whereas there is little place for "aggressive" ones.

Instead of aggression, hatred, and rage, there is ambivalence. She argues that the mother "often awakens her child's ambivalence toward her, and unintentionally brings on its rejection of her and of the care which she has provided."[23] But this "ambivalence" does not include "true hate," which has been excluded a priori from the relation between mother and child in favor of what Chodorow denotes as "confusion" over boundaries and separation.[24] Central to Chodorow's enterprise is her account of the bond between mother and daughter. The daughter forms, and maintains, an "intense ambivalent attachment" to her mother.[25] Yet it seems that even this ambivalence does not include rage and hatred. Chodorow states in commenting upon the unpleasant residues of early emotional life in general:

For my purposes, what is important is that much . . . anxiety, conflict, and ambivalence is not generated endogenously through infantile development, but is an infantile reaction to disruptions and discomforts in its relations with its mother.[26]

Or, in other words, (much) ambivalence stems from remediable difficulties in the relation between child and care giver.[27] What, then, is to be made of the "dramatically intense and ambivalent" lifelong relation between mother and daughter? There are two ways to resolve these arguments. One is that there is no hate, no rage, in "ambivalence." This solution is compatible with Chodorow's critique of Dinnerstein's account of mother-daughter ambivalence. The other resolution is that the passions of the "intense and ambivalent" mother-daughter tie would subside to a considerable degree if "disruptions and discomforts" in the relationship did not occur.

Neither of these resolutions is satisfactory. The latter, in particular, would raise questions about whether (most) girls would continue to become heterosexual, given the role that ambivalence toward mother presumably plays in encouraging girls to switch their object choice from mother to father. In any case, it is questionable that "ambivalence" means in Chodorow's theory what it means for Klein. And this difference, once apprehended as such, can illuminate Chodorow's retreat from a more comprehensive account of rage and hatred.

Ian Craib summarizes the contribution of Klein to psychoanalytic theory as dealing with "the balance of love and hate."[28] This is a far better characterization than the more usual one, namely, that Klein is a theorist of hate or aggression. The balance consists in "the struggle between love and hate, with all the conflicts to which it gives rise, [that] sets in . . . in early infancy, and is active all through life."[29] It is not the absence of conflicting passions but the way that the child (and, later, adult) deals with them that becomes the foundation upon which other relationships and "cultural developments" in the larger world are founded.

The passions do, for Klein, proceed from the life and death drives, a formulation to which many contemporary Kleinians still adhere. They also, however, come from inevitable frustrations, including, as Bion points out, from the frustration of developmentally necessary psychic processes (like projection).[30] This means that when the child is regularly not permitted to create/discover its own meaning in the world (or its own identity) by, for example, externalizing, or projecting, its "bad," hating, aggressive feelings onto another, the result is a *disruption* in the progress of the self, not an "unproblematic" maturation. To the extent that Chodorow suggests that favorable circumstances for relations are prepared in the absence of rage and hatred, she implies that these passions have only a harmful, or maladaptive, role to play in the constitution of the self.

Kleinian theory challenges this perfect congruence between "love" and desirability, "hate" and undesirability. Kleinians maintain that splitting of love and hate, and the assigning of them to different objects, can facilitate the early discriminations between "good" and "bad" that are crucial to the later capacity for judgment. The wider distribution of all emotions to objects beyond the family can assist, according to Klein, the "diffusion" of emotions necessary to the maturation of the power to attempt reparation in the larger world.[31]

For Klein, the expression of hatred is necessary because it encourages the individual to find and protect, to nurture, objects of love, and by so doing assure that the existence of love and goodness can be trusted.[32] The stable acquisition of identity itself depends to some degree, Kleinians contend, on the experience of hatred; this refers to the distinction and delineation of self from not-self, not only originally in relations with parents, but also in relations with siblings and later others.[33] Joan Riviere takes this insight farther, arguing that a need to hate others, to use others as receptacles for our own disavowed hatred and anger, "is one of the main stimuli towards recognizing other people's existence at all."[34]

Similarly, love is regarded more equivocally by Klein than in most, even psychoanalytic, feminist theory. Some skepticism about love (or empathy, concern) as a normative prescription surely results from the belief that love can be a disguise for defensive processes, like idealization (which can be at times functional, at times rigid and destructive). Love can also be experienced as dangerous: for the self, in entailing dependence on another, or to the other, in its vehemence and potential to use the other up.

But even Klein could be suspected of using an ideal of love uncritically. Adam Phillips notes that Winnicott expressed concern with Klein's notion of reparation, believing that it might denote a form of "compliance" to another's demands. In Phillips's words, Winnicott feared that "love" might actually be "more like a protection-racket, a sophisticated version of being nice to mother."[35]

Klein is adamant that the passions are not transcended with maturation. For Kleinian thinkers the ability to sustain ambivalence is an achievement, albeit a sometimes fragile one; it implies the capacity to tolerate and integrate contradictory feelings toward the self and toward others. Ambivalence remains throughout life a central aspect of relations, both private and public. This does not mean that the passions must remain unmodulated as in the very young; they can be altered through learning, experience, and interaction in facilitating environments. And yet they remain, inextricably bound to relations with others, yet potentially disruptive of the objective perception and mature respect that ideally characterize relations.

In "Toward a Relational Individualism: The Mediation of Self Through Psychoanalysis" Chodorow lucidly constructs the difference between orthodox psychoanalytic theory and object relations in their conceptualization of "individualism and the self." It is object relations, she maintains, that provides a way of envisaging the "self that is in its very structure fundamentally implicated in relations with others."[36] This vision of the self is of one that has been formed through the interactions of internal and external object worlds, a self that carries her world with her, to paraphrase Joan Riviere. Chodorow does not, however, write in this essay of conflicting passions except when quoting Riviere:

Other persons are in fact therefore parts of ourselves, not indeed the whole of them but such parts or aspects of them as we had our relations with, and as have thus become parts of us. And we ourselves similarly have and have had effects and influences, intended or not, on all others who have an emotional relation to us, have loved or hated us. We are members one of another.[37]

What object relations thought makes available to feminist theory is a way of constructing selfhood that understands the self as intrinsically social and connected to others; this is the kind of defense of object relations theory that Chodorow has consistently mounted. Object relations also, however, presents the self as impassioned in and through relations. This is true, to one degree or another, of the contributions of all those object relations theorists upon whom Chodorow relies. It is also true of Klein, perhaps in more obvious ways than is true of those theorists, like Winnicott, whose insights Chodorow does employ.

Chodorow concedes that she is troubled by the aggressiveness and rage of the Kleinian view of the person. But ideas like Klein's are important to a theory like Chodorow's. Klein, like Chodorow, envisions the self as coming into being in the context of relations with others, where the constant dialectic between self and other is expressed in the language of emotions. Chodorow emphasizes the difference between this conception of the self-in-relation and a more orthodox psychoanalytic one in her explanation of parenting as less a matter of provision of need satisfaction than as "participation in an interpersonal, diffuse, affective relationship."[38]

Nonetheless, Chodorow's vision of the passions is limited by her attempt to situate the self in its relations with others while simultaneously denying the rage, hatred, and aggressiveness that are as much a consequence of those relations as are the more agreeable passions. Often Chodorow theorizes the emotional roots and complications of gendered selfhood in subtle ways; perhaps just as often, leaving aside her own and others' insights, she does not.

Klein's contribution to psychoanalytic theory has been described only recently, and then briefly, by Chodorow as lying in its "passion-laden, even painful, rawness and immediacy . . . [in its being] more attentive, in an unmediated way, to the emotions and conflicts that relations rooted in gender evoke in the child and in the child within the adult."[39] This description is consistent with the perspective offered in this analysis of the potential contribution of Kleinian thought to feminist theory. It remains for Chodorow to assimilate this perspective into her work.

Jessica Benjamin: The Bonds of Love

Jessica Benjamin has written extensively as a political theorist and a psychoanalyst. Her oeuvre is correspondingly diverse. Prominent in her work, however, has been an analysis of the combined themes of intimacy and power—"the bonds of love." In writing of these themes Benjamin uses object relations literature to explain the deep psychic roots of relations of domination. The following examination will concentrate on the works in which these themes are elaborated.

In 1980 Benjamin published an essay that sketched the parameters of her argument. Selfhood is created through processes of response and "recognition" between self and other that differ by gender. The ramifications of these differences suffuse all aspects of later life, but Benjamin's immediate concern is with the construction of gender relations and (heterosexual) sexuality.

Relying upon psychoanalytic theory and Hegelian philosophy, Benjamin argues that the differentiation of self from (m)other and the recognition of independent selfhood received from the (m)other together structure both the nature of selfhood and of relations between selves. The original differentiation occurs between child and a caretaker who is, more often than not, either the biological mother or another female. Subsequent experience and development involves every person in similar processes with others, both within the family and outside it. Further, differentiation and recognition are processes that affect females and males very differently; the consequence is a situation in which "each gender is able to represent only one aspect of the self-other relationship, either merging or separating, and each gender plays a part in a polarized whole. But neither attains true independence."[40] Individuals are crippled by the outcome of a process that varies predictably by gender.[41]

The focus that Benjamin gives to her study is the following: to analyze the foundations of "the violence of erotic domination," the "fantasy of rational violence," though not necessarily the "flagrant victimization" associated with "hatred and abuse."[42] Benjamin writes, then, not of intimate violence per se, but of the pervasive, largely unconscious state of being associated with relations of domination and submission. She is concerned with a ubiquitous question: Why do people (and especially women) consent to asymmetrical relations of power? But she is more concerned with the elusive answer to another question: Why do people desire and *need* to pursue and maintain such relations? The answers to these (psychological) questions construct a theory of selfhood that, as Benjamin recognizes, has vast political implications.

It is Benjamin's contention that the story of the bonds of love is not told by merely addressing explicit instances of violation and victimization. The theory explains more than physical abuse and overt overtures of hatred. Yet Benjamin discovers rage at the root of the early environmental failures that she investigates—rage that persists in a variety of permutations in the mature forms of selfhood that she analyzes. What is the place of the disagreeable passions in Benjamin's account of the selves created in the bonds of love?

Love, Power, and Rage

At the center of Benjamin's account of masculine domination are issues of differentiation and recognition, and the interrelated issue of individuals' sense of the boundaries between self and other. Benjamin's account here echoes Chodorow's: Masculine developmental dynamics culminate in the construction of rigid boundaries; in women, very different dynamics result in the creation of more elastic boundaries. Adult women and men construct the self-other, subject-object, distinction in incommensurable ways. It is not only intimate relations that are affected by this divergence. Collective, social relations and intellectual endeavors reflect and perpetuate masculine psychic experience:

Both in theory and in practice our culture knows only one form of individuality: the male stance of overdifferentiation, of splitting off and denying the tendencies toward sameness, merging, and reciprocal responsiveness. . . . To be a woman is to be excluded from this rational individualism, to be either an object of it or a threat to it.[43]

Until this point, Benjamin's and Chodorow's analyses are similar. Benjamin, however, additionally relies upon aspects of Hegel's inquiry into the master-slave relation to connect gendered facets of development with broader patterns of relations of domination. These perspectives meet in the analysis of the need for recognition and the costs of failed recognition:

The "paradox of recognition" is this: at the very moment of realizing our own independence, we are dependent upon another to recognize it. At the very moment we come to understand the meaning of "I, myself," we are forced to see the limitations of that self. At the moment when we understand that separate minds can share the same state, we also realize that these minds can disagree.[44]

The self desires to be all there is, and it searches for another who is capable of confirming this. But in order for the other truly to recognize and confirm the self's existence, the other must also be recognized as a self. And each self must renounce its claim to be all there is. There is much room in this dynamic interplay for disruption and deficiency.

"The ideal 'resolution' of the paradox of recognition is for it to continue as a *constant tension*."[45] This would mean that rather than fully subjugating the other to one's own needs, thus losing the other's authentic response, the self is able to confer independent status on the other — to recognize the other's reality. Unfortunately, it is this tension that Benjamin argues is not maintained in early parent-child relations. The failures in this tension are of two varieties. In one scenario, the parent does not maintain the boundary of a true other, the child's will triumphs, and "he" wins—"negation, emptiness [and] isolation."[46] In the other, the parent's boundary is unyielding, the child's will is broken, and "she" learns to give up her will and be compliant.[47] The identification of each scenario of failed recognition with gender is not accidental; as an analyst, Benjamin claims an empirical link consistent enough to create a socially pervasive set of unconscious fantasies.

It is in analyzing the varieties of failure of recognition that Benjamin examines the nature of the disagreeable passions. In the early essay the connections between these are particularly clear.

Rage is a reaction to the other's retreat or the other's retaliation.[48]

For the masochist as well as the sadist, the search is for the other person's boundary as a protection from emptiness and rage.[49]

Both of the responses to the child's search for recognition that Benjamin identifies as deforming have similar emotional consequences. Rage results when the "power struggle" for recognition is thwarted. The original struggle, of course, takes place in the mother-child dyad. But once development is frozen into an impotent struggle, that struggle is repeated throughout life; the repetition and its consequences are the focus of Benjamin's theory.

For each of the scenarios of failed recognition, rage is a result. The characters in the drama of domination and submission use one another to repeat and to cope with their psychic disfigurement and the rage that underlies it. But there is much about the disagreeable passions in Benjamin's theory that is not exhausted by this observation. Scrutiny of the distinction that Benjamin makes between rage and early aggression reveals greater complexity.

Benjamin innovatively applies Donald Winnicott's psychoanalytic thought to clarify the intersubjective dimension of the search for recognition. In Winnicott, as in Benjamin, aggression plays a central role in the self's early, creative relation to the world. It is central to what he terms, somewhat counterintuitively, "destruction." Aggression for both theorists is the self's mode of engagement with the world; it is one medium through which the child "creates" for itself the reality of all that lies beyond itself.[50]

Benjamin's interpretation of Winnicott will be addressed below. What is important here is that Benjamin regards aggression as innocent assertion of the self and as necessary to development, whereas rage is the malignant result of deformed development. How does this distinction emerge? Benjamin contends that rage results only from the failures of recognition that consolidate the fantasy of domination and submission; she thus implies that it can conceivably be eliminated. Rage in this formulation is an unfortunate by-product of dysfunctional relatedness.

When Benjamin does, near the end of *The Bonds of Love*, explicitly address hatred it is in the context of the integration of hate with love in early life.[51] Hatred there is linked to early aggression and, thus, is made a natural and ubiquitous aspect of early development. In juxtaposing hate and love, Benjamin seems to suggest that deep and conflicting passions are endemic to selfhood; this would be consistent with her belief, articulated elsewhere, that "the most intense sense of selfhood involves contradictory feelings."[52]

On the other hand, the arguments that surround aggression, hatred, and rage diverge meaningfully. Only rage (as distinguished from hatred) is a passion that is negative, subversive, malign. Hate and aggression are quintessential to being human, are (in successful development) benign, and further, are transfigured by maturation. This is so because Benjamin identifies aggression with Winnicott's destruction. Her interpretation of Winnicott, then, supports her treatment of the disagreeable passions. To state this conclusion another way, Benjamin's arguments suggest the following: Disagreeable passions in early life, although natural, are not harmful; disagreeable passions in later life, although harmful, are not natural.

At the same time, Benjamin minimizes the importance of fantasy and the "inner world" in her account of early aggression and destruction. The argument suggests that aggression has less of an impact, and certainly a less enduring impact, on inner life than does rage. In fact, Benjamin plays down the intrapsychic dimension of healthy development throughout *The Bonds of Love*. The theory is presented as "intersubjective" theory, to differentiate it from more orthodox psychoanalytic, "internalization" (or "intrapsychic") theory:

I suggest that intrapsychic and intersubjective theory should not be seen in opposition to each other (as they usually are) but as complementary ways of understanding the psyche. To recognize the intersubjective self is not to deny the importance of the intrapsychic: the inner world of fantasy, wish, anxiety, and defense; of bodily symbols and images whose connections defy the ordinary rules of logic and language.[53]

The "inner world" is the focus of intrapsychic theory. This leaves open the issue of how the content of that world will be accounted for in intersubjective theory, because Benjamin states that "it is beyond the scope of [her] discussion to propose a scheme for synthesizing the two approaches."[54] In fact, this difficulty becomes obvious when the issue is the integration of the disagreeable passions into her theory.

There is reasonable consistency in Benjamin's conceptualizations of, especially, aggression and rage. What is troubling about this consistency is the way in which aggression (and perhaps hatred, although this is less clear) is in Benjamin's account drained of its passionate—and affective—intensity. Aggression, in being identified with Winnicott's idea of destruction, is seen as "the wish for absolute assertion of oneself, the demand to have one's own way, the negation of the outside."[55] All this is about the interplay between self and other, not "intrapsychic" reality.

More importantly, all that takes place in the dynamic interplay with the mother subsides in satisfaction when the quest for recognition is successful. The account of aggression that emerges suggests that normal healthy development does not leave residues of unconscious anger and hatred. When aggression is executed successfully, the other is appreciated as a separate person and a sense of reality is acquired.

Benjamin's explicit stance gives a more central role than this to the richness and volatility of unconscious mind: "Without the intrapsychic concept of the unconscious, intersubjective theory becomes one-dimensional, for it is only against the background of the mind's private space that the *real* other stands out in relief."[56] Yet the thrust of her argument is that healthy development substitutes knowledge of otherness, reflectiveness about difference, and respect for the *real* other in place of passions "that defy the ordinary rules of logic." Significantly, it is rage, the only resolutely destructive and unconscious passion of which Benjamin writes, that proceeds from psychic pain and malformation. It is difficult to escape the conclusion that psychic health permits the self to escape from the "inner world" (and especially the negative aspects of that world) whereas psychic trauma dooms the unfortunate to living within it. Benjamin's arguments regarding the disagreeable passions can be explored more critically through an examination of aspects of Winnicott's thought.

Donald Winnicott and Destruction

In mapping the vicissitudes of the bonds of love, Benjamin relies upon the object relations theory of Donald Winnicott. In particular, she relies upon Winnicott's account of destruction, which is embedded in his theory of transitional experience. In Benjamin's appropriation of Winnicott, destruction is, quite generally, the means by which the child comes to discover the existence of an independent other; it is, thus, also the means by which the child is enabled to discover its own independent existence, to consolidate its self. How does Benjamin elaborate these processes?

Especially in her early chapter entitled "Master and Slave," Benjamin remains close to many of Winnicott's arguments. She relates the idea of destruction as involving the child in destroying, or negating, the other in constant fantasy. This, presumably, refers not only to the "no" of the toddler to its parents but also to a more persistent unconscious battle in thought and feeling. The child attacks yet is pleased if the object of repeated attacks survives. Survival signals that the external person is real and beyond the child's omnipotent control; this survival, or lack thereof, constructs, for better or worse, the child's experience of otherness.

The aggression of which Benjamin writes is that entailed by destruction. She cites an imaginary monologue that to Winnicott illustrated the role of aggression in constructing the earliest relationships: " 'Hullo, object!' 'I destroyed you.' 'I love you.' 'You have value for me because of your survival of my destruction of you.' 'While I am loving you I am all the time destroying you in (unconscious) *fantasy.*' "[57] As Winnicott acknowledges, destruction can fail. It is Benjamin's project to pick up where Winnicott left off and to limn the consequences of failure for intimate and social relations, but the foundation provided by Winnicott for Benjamin's project is critical to it. It is Winnicott who incisively describes the psychic dynamics of the struggle to differentiate, and its implications for later relations.

In spite of the apparent faithfulness of Benjamin's appropriation, however, there are problems with her use of Winnicott's theory. First, in the course of presenting his theory as a basis for her own ideas, Benjamin creates a rigid equation in which early failure in destruction causes the substitution of fantasy for reality:

When destruction fails, the aggression goes inside and fuels the sense of omnipotence.[58]

When things are not resolved "out-side," between self and other, the interaction is transferred into the world of fantasy.[59]

Internalization then replaces interaction or exchange with the outside.[60]

Second, Benjamin underestimates the complexity of Winnicott's own ideas regarding hatred and aggression, as in her conclusion that "Winnicott's conception of destruction is innocent."[61] A closer consideration of Winnicott's theory shows that Benjamin's interpretation circumscribes the place of the passions.

Commentators on Winnicott's thought have found in it a model that makes healthy development a function of "good-enough" care and that makes painful and dysfunctional internal experience the consequence of inadequate care. Winnicott's thought has often been attractive to feminists because it emphasizes the significance of external experiences and social arrangements at the same time that it minimizes emphasis on negative emotions.[62] But this is not the only possible interpretation of Winnicott. In fact, there is much in his writings that challenges this interpretation.

Craib suggests that Winnicott's explicit arguments imply, on the one hand, the "possibility of the absence of evil from human life," a view that Craib finds less than plausible.[63] Yet Craib also finds in Winnicott a more "Kleinian" articulation of the problem of ambivalence in human relations that makes Winnicott's understanding of the passions difficult to dismiss as romantic.

In Winnicott's theory of development, most clearly in his version of reparation, he did not see the disagreeable passions merely as relics of early life. Winnicott substituted for such of Klein's formulations as "innate sadism," his own "aggressive non-compliance." Winnicott's language was carefully chosen to reflect theoretical divergence from Klein, yet he believed that in order for the child to discover, or create, the most unique parts of its own being, some other person (or persons) has to be defied and hated. Although the specific early "ruth-less" aggression against the other subsides in the face of maturity and salutary circumstances, all the disagreeable passions do not. This can be seen in his innovative exploration of "transitional space" in which the account of destruction is embedded.

The nuances of Winnicott's theory of transitional space are necessarily lost in a brief discussion. Such a discussion can, however, suggest ways in which the logic of Winnicott's own arguments accounts for the longevity and tenacity of anger, hatred, and aggression. For Winnicott (as for Benjamin), transitional space is that "area of experiencing" that is neither internal to the self (fantasy) nor external (reality). It is something in between, intermediate, what he calls the space of "illusion" and the "place where the secret is." It is in this space that the infant first begins to discover and confront the reality outside; it is in this space that the infant creates and manipulates its own unique contribution to being.

Transitional space is forged through phase-appropriate adaptations of the environment (sometimes, "environment-mother") to the child's needs. Even when adaptation is "good enough" and frustrations are not overwhelming, the need for transitional space does not wane. Transitional space is the space of adult creativity, of the arts, of culture and religion; that which is neither entirely inside the self and unsharable nor objectively perceivable. "The task of reality-acceptance," what is in psychoanalysis often called "reality-testing," is what is negotiated in transitional space. And the disagreeable passions have a role in this space.

Winnicott says of transitional space and the developmental ends that it serves:

It is an area that is not challenged, because no claim is made on its behalf except that it shall exist as a resting-place for the individual engaged in the perpetual human task of keeping inner and outer reality separate yet interrelated.[64]

"Keeping inner and outer reality separate yet interrelated" is an ongoing task, not one that is completed in the individual's earliest relations. What is required for this feat to be achieved is the ability to locate "objects," in this case persons, outside oneself, and to recognize their objective existence in the shared world. This is the process that Winnicott labels "destruction." It is in the logic of Winnicott's arguments that for destruction to succeed, more is required than what Benjamin implies in her interpretation of these events: namely, the early, "good enough" response. In fact, this is the key to the distinction between Winnicott and Benjamin. For Winnicott, the individual must be able to continue to test the survival of the outside world; the very maintenance of a space "between" inner and outer reality depends upon this constant negotiation. Winnicott has this to say about the process between "subject" and "object" (not, meaningfully, between "child" and "mother"):

It is important to note that it is not only that the subject destroys the object because the object is placed outside the area of omnipotent control. It is equally significant to state this the other way round and to say that it is the destruction of the object that places the object outside the area of the subject's omnipotent control. In these ways the object develops its own autonomy and life, and (if it survives) contributes-in to the subject, according to its own properties. In other words, because of the survival of the object, the subject may now have started to live a life in the world of objects, and so the subject stands to gain immeasurably; *but the price has to be paid in acceptance of the ongoing destruction in unconscious fantasy relative to object relating.*[65]

In generalizing the more specific argument regarding early experience, Winnicott here attests both to the enduring quality of destruction and to its affective grasp—"the price to be paid"—on the internal life of the individual. Even in the circumstances when "all goes well," and frustration, despair, loss, and the unresponsiveness of the environment are not too great, there is a continuing necessity to "make objects real." In the realness that constitutes otherness, and therefore assists in constituting the self, objects are "hated as well as loved."[66] In other contexts, either Klein or Winnicott might call this state of affairs ambivalence. Whatever it is named, it is at the root of morality in reparation and at the center of the very process of establishing and maintaining a self in a world of others.

Benjamin's interpretation of Winnicott helps her to construct an account of the disagreeable passions that minimizes their importance in the construction of the self. Because Winnicott himself often sought to minimize the links with Klein, there is support for this interpretation in Winnicott's writings. But there is support as well for an interpretation that is more congruent with Winnicott's struggle to give perspective to the place of the passions, the "destructiveness" that he felt was given "proper emphasis" in the work of Melanie Klein. For Benjamin, destruction does not seem to be an continuing issue in (normal, or healthy) relational life; it also does not engage the life of the mind in the deep sense to which Winnicott's theory alludes.

Conclusion

Nancy Chodorow and Jessica Benjamin have developed unique and provocative theories within the framework of psychoanalytic object relations thought. Both have created new theories on the foundations of object relations. Not only have Chodorow and Benjamin been selective in appropriating from this earlier tradition, but just as importantly, they have been innovative in their approach to these ideas. It is not just that new questions are formulated (although this is certainly true), but that new applications transform the very contours of object relations theory.

In selecting from and transforming the ideas of early object relations theorists, however, Chodorow and Benjamin craft inadequate accounts of the disagreeable passions. In the work of Chodorow, the passions are both present and marginalized. The struggle to construct a normative theory of mature relations in the context of an explanatory account of the formation of gender identity is a complex project. Ultimately, the disagreeable passions are lost in this project. Benjamin does consistently integrate rage and aggression into her account of selfhood, but this integration is problematic in its suggestion that powerful and tenacious disagreeable emotions are the result of dysfunctional developmental dynamics.

The work of Chodorow and Benjamin brings us nearer to understanding the disagreeable passions in the context of relations than does that of Gilligan. But their collective answer to mature social relations is that such relations ideally are negotiated by persons for whom psychic health means freedom from rage, hatred, even abiding ambivalence. This is a very different response to the disagreeable passions than that of another object relations feminist, Dorothy Dinnerstein. Dinnerstein does not promise freedom from the passions; neither does she exculpate individuals for using the passions as motivations to do harm. Dinnerstein does not make the communitarian mistake of inferring malleable, genderless, and one-dimensional selves. She does not compound the error of other object relations feminists by assuming away disagreeable passions in an ideal future.

CHAPTER 5

Reconstituting the Self in Social Theory

Morality and performance of duty are artificial measures that become necessary when something essential is lacking. The more successfully a person was denied access to his or her feelings in childhood, the larger the arsenal of intellectual weapons and the supply of moral prostheses has to be, because morality and a sense of duty are not sources of strength or fruitful soil for genuine affection. . . . But those who have spontaneous feelings can only be themselves. They have no other choice if they want to remain true to themselves.

—Alice Miller,
For Your Own Good

The Disagreeable Passions: A Reprise

We are often tacitly invited by political philosophy to consider a world in which the passions scarcely exist. When theorists do consider the passions and their effects on social life, diverse conclusions emerge: the passions either enhance or thwart convivial social relations and joint political enterprises; the impact of the passions is muted by the regularizing processes of the economic marketplace;[1] certain passions are more socially functional—and, in an extraordinary coincidence, more natural—among certain kinds of persons. All these and many other observations are available to the student of political thought.

What feminists consistently have done is question the veracity and normative force of social theories in which women and childhood do not appear. The subversive practice of placing women, childhood, and thus,

93

inescapably, developmental issues at the center of social theories has yielded new answers about the nature of the self. More important, perhaps, it has yielded new questions.

In evaluating and using the work of such communitarians as Michael Sandel, Alasdair MacIntyre, and others, many feminists have taken at face value and incorporated the claims that these theorists have made. Communitarian theorists have criticized the ahistorical, rationalistic, and transcendent, ultimately singular "self" and claimed to put in its place a connected, embedded, contextual multiplicity of "selves." The affinity of communitarian to feminist thought appears patent. And yet, on closer examination, the communitarian promise runs aground; the resistance to issues of fear, vulnerability, hostility, envy, and even love, brings into question the communitarian commitment to accounting for human particularity.

What does it mean to suggest that the feminist inclusion of women, childhood, and internal life poses new questions for social theory? Philosopher Sara Ruddick observes that the mother "must be realistic about the psyche whose growth she fosters" because "*all* psyches are moved by fear, lust, anger, pride, and defenses against them."[2] Psychoanalyst Alice Miller is similarly descriptive, but not merely so. For her, the fact that all psyches are prone to human frustration, conflict, discontent, and the emotions related to them is only the nascent part of a critique, both of modes of child rearing and of social relations. Miller writes of the denial and suppression, especially in children, of emotions that are unwanted by adult care givers. "The lost world of feelings" is one in which the passions that are not permitted or tolerated can no longer be experienced; envy, anger, anxiety are disclaimed and, thus, lost to the self.[3] Miller claims that authenticity and the capacity to be a complete moral actor depend upon more than the mutuality of love, care, and affection, although these are indispensable.

Feminist psycho-social theories have injected sophisticated psychological description into debates about developmental and relational struggles. The order in which these theories are presented here is not random. From Gilligan, through Chodorow and Benjamin, to Dinnerstein, these theories explore deeper, less conscious, and, not surprisingly, more disturbing aspects of selves and relations. The last of these, Dorothy Dinnerstein's theory of gender relations, remains one of the bleaker accounts precisely because of her refusal to banish the disagreeable passions.

Dorothy Dinnerstein

Since its publication in 1976, *The Mermaid and the Minotaur* has had a dramatic effect on contemporary feminist thought. Both Dinnerstein's provocative language and her controversial theses have been criticized extensively by some feminists, even as the work has been lauded by others. Some reasons for an ambivalent reception are not hard to find.

First, in claiming to disclose our most urgent individual and collective problem, Dinnerstein indicts current gender, familial, and social arrangements relentlessly while leaving intact normative assumptions about heterosexuality and the virtues of the nuclear family. Second, she assumes the continuity of infant and adult emotional states, the essential resistance of emotional life to maturity and the passage of time, in a way that defies much wish and popular-psychological wisdom. Third, she fails to theorize adequately the sources of women's resistance to the dynamics that she exposes, even though she notes that women have resisted and continue to do so. Finally, she locates responsibility for the compulsive destructiveness of personal and social life in both men's behavior and women's complicity, making both sexes culpable.

Dinnerstein's project is an attempt to locate the roots of "human malaise," including destructive orientations toward ourselves, others, and the natural world, in early patterns of nurturance and psychological life. She reminds readers that "primary female responsibility for the care of infants and young children" has been a "core fact" of human arrangements across societies and historical periods.[4] But, more important than this brute fact are its implications—in human imagination and response, in our capacities for forming bonds and resisting them, in the contours of emotional being and action. "Woman-dominated child care" is the "primitive cornerstone of human solidarity" and simultaneously the "primitive cornerstone of human pathology."[5]

Female-dominated child care produces offspring that are "semi-human, monstrous." It produces children (and thus adults) who use the entrenched and gendered division of labor to evade much of the pain involved in development and who are, thus, dangerously deformed. How does female-dominated child care produce this result? Because a woman is the "will's first, overwhelming adversary"[6] and the object of the most primitive passions, "Woman" becomes, for both women and men, a category of preternatural creature; "she" must be subdued, denied, recanted, controlled, debased—even as she is being loved, desired, and feared.[7] Healthy (i.e., nondestructive) intimate and social existence waits for a time when people will have outgrown the need to dodge the demands of maturity and will voluntarily change what appear to most to be natural gender and social arrangements. New arrangements will have as their basis shared parenting of children by members of both sexes.

Dinnerstein does not employ an exclusively psychoanalytic paradigm. Perspectives and evidence from social psychology, anthropology, and philosophy contribute to the case that Dinnerstein makes for the need to redistribute the tasks of child care. In any case, despite the ways in which Dinnerstein's concerns are linked to maternity, mortality, and even the Freudian "drives,"[8] the argument is not a biological one; Dinnerstein's interest is in the emotional ramifications of social arrangements and in the further social ramifications of these emotional needs and patterns. To elucidate these connections she relies upon object relations theory, and especially the work of Melanie Klein.

Dinnerstein, like Klein, is particularly attentive to the reverberations of early feeling throughout life. Dinnerstein has been criticized for the "unrigorous" style of argumentation that she adopts. The "emotive" character of her work, it is charged, distracts from its message.[9] Yet it is this style that points to what she captures and reproduces most profoundly: "the way in which adult feeling resonates with the emotional atmosphere of infancy."[10]

But this in itself does not speak to the issue of the tractability of these feelings. What is the nature of the disagreeable emotions in Dinnerstein's argument? Much of her theory rests on an assumption that rage, hatred, fear, and anxiety are an ineradicable part of the human condition. They are in large measure the products of either innate dispositions or of frustrations, deprivations, and inconsistencies of nature and nurturance that lie (in present conditions, and perhaps in any conditions) beyond the scope of human will and manipulation:

The early mother, monolithic representative of nature, is a source, like nature, of ultimate distress as well as ultimate joy. Like nature, she is both nurturing and disappointing, both alluring and threatening, both comforting and unreliable.[11]

Occasionally Dinnerstein does seem to suggest that destructive gender arrangements themselves are the cause of "pain and hate" in the world.[12] But this is not the position that is most consistent with her theory. A better formulation integrates these arguments: disagreeable passions are constituted in a variety of ways, including as a consequence of alienating, divisive, and scapegoating gender relations. This rendering of her argument clarifies that, although we would be better off without our current arrangements, these changes alone would not free us from the necessity of struggling with troubling passions and their consequences.

The Persistence of the Passions

Dinnerstein's arguments culminate in an ostensibly simple conclusion: Women and men should share the responsibilities of child rearing. Perhaps it is because of this seeming simplicity that their complexity has not always been adequately appreciated. Of course this "complexity" is a function not only of the arguments themselves. It is also a function of the features of the social and economic milieu that make traditional child-rearing arrangements seem necessary, natural, and unalterable. Neither can a complete account of these arguments be given here, but certain themes can be examined in more detail to discover the place of the disagreeable passions in Dinnerstein's theory.

Of the (potentially) disagreeable and hurtful nature of the self Dinnerstein has much to say: "All of us have some cruel, coercive, destructive impulses toward other people."[13] Although she argues that these impulses are far less acceptable in women than in men, thus accounting for much of the divergence in their expression, she does not make them solely the result of misshapen gender arrangements. Prelinguistic feelings surrounding pleasure, dependence, helplessness, gratitude, and resentment of the body and its limitations and frustrations, among other causes, contribute to a reservoir of emotions that resonate over the life span "with the atmosphere of our very early emotional life."[14] Dinnerstein emphasizes the role of envy, along with defenses against envy.

In her foundational work, *Envy and Gratitude,* Melanie Klein defines envy as one kind of "destructive impulse." Dinnerstein follows Klein in conceptualizing envy as a form of "destructive rage" with particular ontogenic features and consequences.[15] Envy is of all the emotions uniquely influential "on the development of the capacity for gratitude and happiness" or, as Klein also puts it, on the individual's "capacity for love and goodness."[16] This is because envy is an assault on connection, and on the possibility of the survival of goodness. It is also because envy begets envy; as the intensity and persistence of envy increase, the possibilities for respite and repair decline.

Klein's analysis of envy discloses much about her account of infantile mental life. From the beginning of life primitive object relations exist, as does an immature ego. The child engages, virtually from birth, in splitting and keeping apart perceptions and phantasies connected to its experiences. Splitting—usually of "good" and "bad," though sometimes along other dimensions—is necessary to mental development, helping to constitute the core of later, more mature, discriminations between "goodness" and "badness." The nascent ego maintains good and bad images and phantasies of self and the outside world separate in consciousness. Hence, splitting both facilitates envy, by giving envious feelings "goodness" as a target, and acts as a defense against envy, by working in the service of attempts to preserve that very goodness.

The inchoate realization that the source of nourishment, gratification—in fact, of goodness itself—is outside the self and beyond the self's control is the catalyst of envy. Why should this realization inevitably result in destructive, rather than predominantly conciliatory and loving, impulses? Klein's answer to this question is that the object is hated and assaulted not in spite of, but because of its goodness.

Envy is the angry feeling that another person possesses and enjoys something desirable—the envious impulse being to take it away or spoil it.[17]

There are very pertinent psychological reasons why envy ranks among the seven "deadly sins." I would even suggest that it is unconsciously felt to be the greatest sin of all, because it spoils and harms the good object which is the source of life.[18]

The helpless dependence that all humans experience spawns intense and contradictory feelings about the inability to control and possess "goodness."

However, phantasied assaults on what is perceived to be good—the mother, or perhaps a part of her—are experienced as unbearable. The consequence is phantasied persecution: the source of goodness is transformed into a source of harm. The consequences of envy join with the unavoidable deprivations and delays in care and nurturance to exacerbate the infant's anxiety. As a result, the "phantasy of an inexhaustible breast," the internalized soothing representation of fulfillment and nurturance, is suffused with ominous significance. That which was experienced (and attacked) as good, externally and then internally, becomes bad; additionally, it becomes the source and paradigm of "badness." As Dinnerstein puts it, relating this general argument to the blaming of women, "The mother, then—like nature, which sends blizzards and locusts as well as sunshine and strawberries—is perceived as capricious, [and] sometimes actively malevolent."[19] Once the source of goodness is endangered, the destruction of internal and external badness in phantasy, feeling, and, later, action, feels warranted by the necessity for self-preservation. Splitting thus can occasion more and more rigid splitting in an attempt to protect some goodness within and without. And this fragile compromise remains throughout life to threaten the possibility of a "realistic" response to the world.

The concept of splitting has been the subject of debate among Kleinian thinkers as well as between Kleinians and others. Jessica Benjamin uses the concept of splitting extensively in her explanation of relations of domination and submission. However, it is Dinnerstein who not only uses the concept in a way that is more consistent with the object relations theory that she interprets, but also in a way that attends to the inevitability of the passions.

Dinnerstein has been criticized for the way she translates the internal dynamics of splitting into social outcomes. C. Fred Alford[20] argues that in Dinnerstein's theory consciousness splits too neatly along the lines of gender. The assigning of good and bad respectively to men and women makes consciousness a perfect mirror image of social life; it does not account for the labile and fragmenting dimensions of a consciousness whose laws are not those of social discourse.

Dinnerstein's retrieval of the disagreeable emotions is not at issue in this criticism, but one response to the criticism can help to clarify the nature of her argument about the passions. In spite of Dinnerstein's failure to consider the full range of possibilities of the consequences of splitting, her theory does not necessarily deny its fluidity. Her theory could responsibly be read to argue that *one* split, between female and male (or like mother and not like mother), has dramatic consequences in part because of the ways in which the split is maintained, indeed coercively enforced, by culture and society. This reading does not invalidate Dinnerstein's reliance on object relations insights. This is so because, even though she focuses on gender, she does not claim that splitting only operates to keep apart images related to gender. The rigidity with which this split (between like mother and not like mother) is maintained socially maintains the possibility in consciousness and social reality that other splits will be fostered. Retaining women as socially sanctioned recipients of rage, envy, hatred, and devaluation "encourages people to indulge the need . . . to embrace other victims as well."[21] And this is so because any such retention of a ready container for the disagreeable passions discourages the emotional pain and growth associated with mature object relations.

It is not incidental that the perceptions and epithets applied to members of hated and devalued groups of men echo and parody those directed by men (and often, as Dinnerstein points out, by women) at women. As many feminists have acknowledged, no unproblematic identity exists between biological sex and unconscious perceptions and fantasies linked to gender. Frantz Fanon,[22] for example, writes eloquently of the characteristics associated with black men in the minds of white men: masochism, passivity, dirt and biological need, sexual voraciousness, primitiveness. All of these are stereotyped fantasies of "the feminine" applied to male "others." Fear and hatred of lesbians and gay men provides an illustration not only of the flexibility of the objects of splitting but also of the fragmentation in perception that splitting can facilitate. Those who sanction the hating of lesbians and gay men do so by asserting consistently that it is not the people themselves that are hated but only the behaviors in which they engage, as though these constituted easily distinguishable units of being. That gay men are vilified as ersatz women is by now a redundant observation.

Dinnerstein's analysis, despite its exclusive focus on gender, does not preclude a sophisticated grasp of the analytic concept of splitting. But an account of rage and hatred in Dinnerstein's work is incomplete unless it adds to a Kleinian conception of splitting a description of the role of projective mechanisms in creating reality.

Projective processes are central to Dinnerstein's theory of gender.

Her core argument is that human beings routinely project onto mother, and by extension women, a specifiable set of human attributes and motives. These then sanctify and necessitate phantasies and acts of aggression and containment against the mother and (later) her surrogates.

To be more precise, Kleinian theorists speak of "projective identification," regarded today as one of Klein's most important contributions to psychoanalytic theory. As Elizabeth Bott Spillius explains it, projective identification occurs "as a phantasy in which bad parts of the self [are] split off from the rest of the self . . . go into an object, and . . . distort the perception of the object."[23] Kleinians stress, as does Dinnerstein, that some degree of projective identification is normal.[24] It can facilitate (although it can also retard) learning about the other; it can be a means to communicate feelings to the other; it can serve as a way of controlling or manipulating the other. Especially in the last respect, projective identification is distinguished from other psychological processes and defenses in the way that it can actually help to structure the feelings and phantasies of a person who is the object of another's projection.

Dinnerstein's focus is on the ways in which both men and women use women as targets for rage and hatred. She points out that hatred directed in "normal" ways at women remains invisible as hatred:

The hate, fear, loathing, contempt, and greed that men express toward women so pervade the human atmosphere that we breathe them as casually as the city child breathes smog. Men who express these feelings in the conventional ways are not thought of as woman-haters. But women who note, however mildly, that this is happening are quickly (in tones of heavy blame which imply that they have disqualified themselves as mentally balanced observers) dismissed as man-haters.[25]

In exploring the particular kind of rage known as "envy" Dinnerstein makes it a human problem. No longer is envy a female complaint, a sign of biological inferiority as in the "penis envy" attributed by Freud to all women. Rather than being gendered, it is understood as a form of response to the outside world, subject to a multiplicity of forms and resolutions. As Jessica Benjamin points out, the denial of male envy of "mother's goodness" can lead men to deny that goodness and to commandeer and control it in other women.[26]

Jane Flax argues that Dinnerstein captures well both the power of unconscious desire and the continuity of infantile and adult passion.[27] In these areas Dinnerstein can be compared with Klein, whose ideas, it is said, "brought to life the infant in us."[28] Flax also argues, however, that Dinnerstein errs in defining both the problem that she relates and its solution in an ahistorical and abstract fashion. The form of the family has not always been the same; neither have social institutions and consciousness remained unchanged over time. Acknowledging the justice of these criticisms requires narrowing the explanatory claims of Dinnerstein's theory. It means suggesting that in modern, middle-class nuclear families the particular patterns that Dinnerstein analyzes might prevail. But the consideration of Dinnerstein's work undertaken here suggests another perspective. If Dinnerstein's application of Kleinian ideas is fruitful for feminist theory, it is rather in the ways that Dinnerstein does not flinch from presenting the intractable character of the disagreeable passions.

The accomplishment of Dinnerstein's theory is in its refusal to redefine the nature of human connection in terms of pure affection, empathy, or love. In spite of its prescriptions about child care, which have as their goal a redistribution of rage between women and men, the theory does not suggest that rearranging social practices would dispel rage and hatred. Dinnerstein argues more conservatively that greater integration of the passions and greater ambivalence might be achieved, first between the sexes, and perhaps concomitantly among other social groups.

Yet one need not accept Dinnerstein's conclusions to see the ways in which her theory contributes to an understanding of the passions. Other conclusions (as well as other, perhaps new, problems) regarding familial and social arrangements might be consistent with Dinnerstein's account of the passions. This account of the passions is simply more adequate than many found in contemporary feminist social theories. Dinnerstein does not assume the easy amelioration of hatred and rage; she does not make them entirely masculine (although they appear most strikingly in men); she does not make them, in women, merely the conscious response to oppression.

One question about Dinnerstein's theory is particularly critical. Janet Sayers maintains that Dinnerstein does not adequately account for women's resistance to male authority, given her argument that women and men accept this authority as a protection from the unmediated power of the mother.[29] Another way of stating this criticism is to say that

Dinnerstein does not account for the turning of female rage and fear away from early care givers and toward social inequality and gender-based oppression. If the disagreeable passions are, as Dinnerstein claims, a part of the human condition, and if our social arrangements facilitate their being aimed predominantly at women, how can women's resistance be accounted for?

It is ironic that Sayers finds in this question a dilemma that challenges the cogency of Dinnerstein's theory; for it is Sayers's critique of Gilligan (chapter 3, above) that Gilligan fails to integrate into her theory of women's psychology the possibility of "contrary intentions" or, more broadly, the fluid and contradictory nature of emotion. In light of this, perhaps the case against Dinnerstein's account of the distribution of the disagreeable passions could with more promise be regarded as too rigid. The criticism would then be that the theory does not encompass the disconcerting reality of rage directed simultaneously at nonidentical targets—for example, both at early care givers and at male violence and domination. This critique would recognize Dinnerstein's contribution to an analysis of the role of disagreeable passions, while encouraging work on understanding the translation of these passions into the anger that helps to fuel feminism.

Splitting in Feminist Theory

Carol Gilligan, Nancy Chodorow, and Jessica Benjamin have (in differing degrees) found in the work of psychoanalyst Donald Winnicott a caring sensibility, an aversion to hatred and aggression, and a sanguine conceptualization of intersubjectivity. Unfortunately, they largely ignore the other discourse of even Winnicott's object relational theory. This is the story of rage and hatred—the story of how the passions are intrinsic to every life.

Carol Gilligan recognizes the "problem of aggression" as one that every person confronts, yet she also defines it as "the intent of one person to hurt another." Perhaps this segue explains much of the general refusal to confront the disagreeable passions: if rage and hate are merely potential violence, violence looking for an object, then acknowledging them might appear tantamount to sanctioning (or at least inviting) violence. And yet it is not true for object relations (or, more generally, psychoanalytic) theorists that speaking about disagreeable passions implies the sanctioning of violence. In the words of Robert Jay Lifton, "anger and rage, along with their violent imagery, [are] painful and often problematic but also at times useful and even, within limits, appropriate. Violent actions, however, [are] harmful and to be avoided."[30]

The work of Winnicott is often, in feminist applications of psychoanalytic theory, given precedence over that of Melanie Klein. In analyzing the precursors of feminist psychoanalytic theory, it is possible to posit a connection between Winnicott's relative popularity among feminists and Klein's relative unpopularity among these same feminists. Klein's reputed overemphasis on rage and aggression informs virtually every reference to her work in feminist psycho-social theory. It is the gentler Winnicott, a man described as a "madonna," whose ideas are more readily appropriated.[31]

This distinction is at least partially illusory and, in fact, operates as a strategy within feminist psycho-social theories. Obviously a purpose has been served by this split between the "good" Winnicott and the "bad" Klein. Feminist theorists have been able to use the considerable insights of psychoanalytic object relations theory while ignoring the emphasis in object relations thought on disagreeable passions. However, this strategy has exacted a price; it has entailed a dichotomization of the passions within a large and important body of feminist theory. In assigning disagreeable ones to Klein (and her followers), and agreeable ones—or the possibility of transcending the disagreeable—to Winnicott, some feminist theorists have abdicated responsibility for struggling with this difficult issue. This strategy mystifies the account of the disagreeable passions in Winnicott's work even as it makes the insights of Klein and those identified with her unavailable to feminist discourse about social relations.

Acknowledgment of disagreeable passions, at the personal, social, and theoretical levels, creates possibilities for discourse about human creativeness and destructiveness. Such acknowledgment helps in other ways: in enlarging the scope of reflection about motives for feeling and action; in aiding the ability to resist the urge to assign hate and rage only to certain groups; in helping to create the preconditions for empathic responsiveness and repair as for angry responsiveness at injustice. It may not be the case that gaining access to the passions would guarantee the mastery of all these capacities. But mastery may not be possible if access to the passions is denied.

Communitarianism Revisited

Many feminists grant that our theories and practices are rooted in and shaped by, among other things, personal experience, the stable and the quixotic aspects of personal identity, and emotional commitments to individuals, groups, symbols, and ideals. Such an understanding necessarily impels feminists to re-cognize the assumptions of social theories. One example of this is feminist attention to gender. Social theories too often do not accommodate themselves easily (or at all) to the possibilities of gender (or other) differences among people; they too often describe "people" while taking some conception of maleness as norm. The consequence of this is a perpetuation of the awkward fit between forms of knowledge about the self and visions of social and political improvement.

Communitarianism actively seeks to constitute real selves in meaningful social contexts, to do justice to the lives that people lead. Yet in the absence of attention to gender, passion, and the development of identity, those aspects of being by means of which the self is constituted and embodied, there is no legitimate account of the self. Communitarian theory does not question how people come to assume particular identities or are positioned to respond to certain role requirements in the ways that communities demand. Communitarians do not generally inquire deeply into the consequences of forms of child rearing. These questions are crucial to feminists, who have been responsible for articulating the ways in which the gender identity and role requirements of communities diminish, burden, and harm women.

Insisting upon the inclusion in social theory of human-developmental processes and the passions that are intrinsic to them is transformative. It is no longer possible to ignore superficial depictions of family relations that do not represent them as engaging and shaping the most tenacious and constitutive aspects of identity. It is no longer possible to deny the ways in which aspects of individual and group feeling and identity contribute to the ideological and institutional construction of social life.

More specifically, one aspect of communitarian thought that has disturbed feminist political theorists is its blindness to the exclusive, coercive, exploitative, and sometimes actively malevolent character of actual communities. This strange blindness on the part of communitarians is more nearly comprehensible in the light of a characterization of the communitarian self as "community writ small."[32] Here the abstract, functional, and ethically benevolent (or neutral) community finds its theoretical counterpart in a self that is not insecure, ambivalent, hating, and loving. This is not a suggestion that the political community should be understood as the self writ large, with a more thick and psychologically adequate self replacing the one that is criticized; it is a suggestion that it is easier for theorists to remain sanguine about the nature of communities when the passions of the selves that inhabit them are presumed away.

A relational social theory that propounds a constitutive view of the self requires a psychology that is not sparse and intuitive. Without such a coherent psychology theorists are left to indulge whatever conceptions of persons fit with their larger designs, or comfort themselves or their audience. Psychoanalytic object relations is consistent with the concerns of relational social theory in important respects. Object relations theory has not been noted for attention to gender development; indeed, the difference between Freud and object relations theorists on the subject is immense. What object relations theorists do contribute is a conceptualization of selves (female and male) as active negotiators and creators. The self is not a solitary receptacle of drives but a subject constituted in the interstices between needs and feelings and the frustrations and demands of a world of others. The processes of identity formation described by object relations theorists such as Klein and Winnicott are lifelong processes, ways in which the self creates meaning, contends with reality, and maintains a sense of its own continuity.

Object relations feminists locate these processes in the acquisition of gender identity, thereby enriching and expanding the descriptive reach of object relations. Using the insights of object relations, feminists identify divergent modes of self formation. Yet it is too often an unintended result of theorizing about gender that positive, mature forms of connection have been predicated exclusively on the human capacity for positive and agreeable emotions. This outcome is at odds with object relations theory; it also fits uneasily with actual intimate and social experience.

Psycho-Social Theory Revisited

The challenge to feminist theory, the necessity to grapple with the disagreeable passions, follows closely upon the feminist enterprise of reconceptualizing the nature of the self to include such aspects of human being as emotion, nurturance, and affiliativeness. It is the invisible, forgotten half of much of the feminist critique. From this perspective, Gilligan, Chodorow, Benjamin, and Dinnerstein can be understood as engaged in a common project: the reconciliation of dominant discourses about the self with women's knowledge, women's concerns, and women's life stories. The foregoing critique represents an attempt to enhance and deepen this reconciliation.

What are the implications for each of these theories of this critique? Two things must be considered before it is possible to answer: first, as the substance and theoretical origins of the theories are diverse, the implications for each theory are necessarily different; second, as the critique represents the nascent part of a process, the implications suggested must be exploratory rather than definitive.

Carol Gilligan is the only one of the theorists examined who rejects the usefulness, indeed, the legitimacy, of a psychoanalytic paradigm. Gilligan listens to her subjects, creating from their narratives (or "intellectual reflections") a meta-narrative of love, empathy, and care which, as critics have pointed out, is absent recognition of the disagreeable passions. Some culpability for this exclusion rests, as N. Katherine Hayles argues, with Gilligan's meta-narrative—with her interpretive reconstruction of women's words. Much is no doubt due to her subjects' suppression of their own, disavowed, emotions.

Yet in spite of this, it cannot be denied that women readers of Gilligan's work have responded with recognition to her depiction of women's moral thinking. All women experience the degrading and disregard of their capacities, and it is the valuing of these capacities for which Gilligan's work is rightly celebrated. The problem is that Gilligan's techniques, as powerful as they are in many respects, can only account for what women (or men) know and can safely articulate. Particularly in the case of women, the assumption that those whose rage has been denied can claim and express it cannot be automatically granted.

Gilligan could account for conscious experiences of anger, rage, and hatred within the parameters of her technique and theory. There is no reason entailed by her research designs for disagreeable passions to be excluded. What is less likely is that she can account for the origins and developmental trajectories of such passions within the constraints of her theory. And it is not clear from her published writings that Gilligan wishes to pursue this avenue of inquiry. Gilligan's position throughout her numerous writings is that disagreeable passions in women stem from relational disconnection and explicable harms. Surely, these assumptions are not at issue; it is possible to grant them and still not accept that the subject is exhausted by them. In the end, Gilligan's equation of care and love with connection and more disagreeable affect with relational disconnection nurtures a facile account of the self. This is a perilous assumption for social theorists.

The work of Nancy Chodorow has provided the foundations for much recent feminist thought. It has, in fact, become identified by many, both friends and critics alike, not as a species of object relations theory but as object relations theory itself. This equation is problematic even though it is unquestionable that Chodorow's work has been a major impetus of feminist research into gender difference. Chodorow appropriates aspects of object relations theory, relying selectively on the work of many pioneers and, at the same time, excluding much. She tells a story of women's greater receptiveness to affiliation, and deeper empathy, with others. She suggests, though not as resolutely as Gilligan, that women's experience of disagreeable passions is derivative of harm.

For the most part, Chodorow merely avoids the disagreeable passions. When they are not avoided, hatred and rage are defined away, as, for example, when hatred becomes the child's "confusion." Chodorow and Benjamin separately criticize Dorothy Dinnerstein for failing to understand the extent to which the social powerlessness of women, hence of "the mother," condition the mother-child relation for failure and, thus, for rage. No feminist would deny that women's subordination affects the processes of mothering, as it affects every social relation. Yet this criticism, along with a failure to theorize about the disagreeable passions, ends by suggesting that women's powerlessness is the only significant cause of hatred and rage. Unfortunately, this implication is not explicitly contradicted.

Jessica Benjamin's exegesis of the psychic story behind the bonds of love is, like Chodorow's, a theory of gender difference. Benjamin relies upon a Winnicottian version of object relations theory to buttress her argument about the different psychic boundaries established by women and men and their implications for the experience of disagreeable passions. In Benjamin's account, rage is a consequence of developmental failure, a sign that something has gone awry in the early psychological process of differentiation from care givers. Her interpretation of Winnicott supports this account; it is merely that Benjamin's reading of Winnicott follows a standard interpretation of his repudiation of disagreeable passions—one that does not inquire into his continuities with a more Kleinian account of the passions.

There are important implications for Benjamin's theory. Associated with Benjamin's assumption that disagreeable passions can dissipate in maturity without residue is her increasingly facile account of internal life. In the course of her argument, "fantasy" and "reality" become rigidly dichotomized, even as Benjamin alludes to the dysfunctional dichotomizing of work (as the world of instrumental rationality and control), and home (as the world of nurturance and intimacy).

The mental operation of splitting that is so subtle a description of mental life when employed by Klein becomes in Benjamin's treatment a way of identifying the successful acquisition of maturity. For Benjamin, the person for whom early aggression has worked properly abandons disagreeable passions in exchange for the ability to split reality from fantasy. The result is that whatever can be learned from Benjamin's interpretation of relations of domination and submission, the possibility of a continuing drama of rage and hatred in optimal development is not integrated into her theory.

It remains to turn again to the theory of Dorothy Dinnerstein, criticized widely for its pessimism about the ubiquity of rage. Dinnerstein's book is usually read as a manifesto for shared parenting; it is this, but it is also more. Dinnerstein contends that the disagreeable passions are, like the capacity for love, part of our endowment as human beings. It is what we do with them—how we claim them (or fail to), how we flee from them, how we attribute them to others—that is at issue. It is clear that Dinnerstein's willingness to engage a set of problems for which simple benevolence and discourse offer no quick solutions is itself laudable. Her troubling depiction of the nature of the self has much to offer to social theories of all descriptions.

Inscribed in the theories of Carol Gilligan, Nancy Chodorow, and Jessica Benjamin is the belief in the capability of human beings in good, empathic, "facilitating," relational environments to transcend disagreeable passions. It is not surprising that, with such a starting point, theorists find what they are looking for—evidence that these passions are unnatural and unnecessary. Is it possible for different assumptions to be incorporated into these influential feminist theories? A tentative suggestion is that this might be more possible in the context of the work of Nancy Chodorow than with that of either Gilligan or Benjamin.

The reason for this has already been alluded to in the discussion of Chodorow's theory in chapter 4. Chodorow's work can be seen as characterized by a high degree of disruption and discontinuity. She both does, and does not, take seriously the core insights of early object relations theory about the psychic processes that help to constitute selves. She is often subtle in speculating about the nature of the relation between mother and daughter, although she abandons many of her own insights in favor of more didactic commentary when she turns to speaking of mature social relations. It might be possible to breach discontinuities like these, not to restore a more "correct" object relational mode of explanation, but to restore the passions.

Gilligan and Benjamin, on the other hand, are more consistent in their assumption, and conclusion, about the nature of disagreeable passions. This consistency of explanation leaves fewer gaps, is more total and seamless; as a result, there is far less probability that insights excised from their respective theories can be incorporated. This does not, of course, deny the substantial contributions of these theories. It does suggest the unlikelihood that they will enhance our understanding of many dimensions of the disagreeable passions.

Whole Selves in Social Theory

Object relations theory provides a set of conceptual tools for strengthening the depth and coherence of social theories. Early object relations theories are rich in analysis of the roots of human interaction—the psychic drama of selves in relation. In important respects, feminist theorists are the heirs to this psychoanalytic tradition, expanding and enriching it beyond the boundaries of mere analytic discourse. Yet there is something that feminists, accustomed to the theories of Chodorow, Benjamin, and Dinnerstein, often forget: Object relations and feminist object relations are not identical. Feminist object relations is both more ambitious and more circumscribed than its (among feminists) lesser known predecessor tradition.

Feminist theorists, having often used object relations theory in exciting new ways, should attend more critically to intellectual roots. There is more at stake in this than the creation of a responsible intellectual history of feminist ideas. Feminist psycho-social theorists have often excised or distorted the place of disagreeable passions in relations. These constructions have obviously helped to shape the concerns and conclusions of theory. There is, however, another consideration. The work of feminist psycho-social theorists has contributed to the reconceptualization of theory in a wide range of disciplines and fields of study, including philosophy, anthropology, literary criticism, political science, education, sociology, history, and the biological sciences. Without a constant willingness to critique interpretive strategies and authorial choices, feminist object relations risks constructing a discourse about human relations that is likely to be uncritically adopted across the disciplines.

What would more self-critical feminist object relations theories look like? The conclusion put forth here is that such theories would incorporate the developmental theory of Melanie Klein, because it is in Klein that the undesirable and disagreeable aspects of human relations command sustained examination. This is not to suggest that an uncritical acceptance of Kleinian ideas is preferable to the relative silence about these ideas that persists among feminist theorists. Klein and her more recent followers should not be installed as the new arbiters of human nature in social theory. On the other hand, the more or less consistent substitution of depictions of human nature as relational (when this implies good, gratifying, benign) rather than individualistic (when this implies bad, painful, corrosive) suggests that some countervailing ideas are necessary.

Not surprisingly, Kleinian object relations theory has furnished the basis for different varieties of social theory. Dinnerstein's remains the germinal application in feminist theory. Two other works are not feminist in orientation, but they offer useful illustrations to inform feminist object relations. Vamik Volkan uses the psychoanalytic theory of Otto Kernberg as foundation for a psychodynamic vision of international politics in *The Need to Have Enemies and Allies*.[33] In Volkan's appropriation of object relations theory, the psychic processes of projection, displacement, and what Volkan terms "externalization" are crucial to the construction of adult enemies and allies in the national and international arenas.[34]

By contrast, C. Fred Alford does not apply object relations theory to particular conflicts (Volkan illustrates his arguments, for example, with reference to the struggles between Cypriot Greeks and Cypriot Turks). Alford's project is the recasting of Klein's individual psychology into a group psychology that is adequate to address, among other issues, the "discrepancy between individual and group morality."[35] Thus, although some overlap exists in the concerns of all three theorists, and especially for present purposes in the willingness of all three to confront the disquieting relational consequences of disagreeable passions, differences remain. Dinnerstein addresses gender relations, Volkan, international relations, and Alford, a Kleinian theory of groups. The range of possible uses of a robust object relations theory is not difficult to envision.

Given the fascinating uses to which Winnicott's psychoanalytic ideas have been put by feminists, there is ample reason to believe that a Winnicottian object relations approach is fruitful for feminist social thought. There are substantive intellectual differences, as well as differences of style and emphasis, between Winnicott and Klein, as there are among present-day self-described Kleinians. However, the distinction that has allowed feminists to choose Winnicott over Klein when selecting psychoanalytic ideas obscures a dimension of Winnicott's work that social theorists ignore at their peril. Winnicott and Klein do not represent opposite theoretic poles on some continuum of belief in individual and relational goodness.

Conclusion

Feminist psycho-social theories do not speak with a single voice on the subject of women's hatred and rage. Nevertheless, a dominant theme emerges, one that accounts for women by reiterating certain aspects of female socialization. Do feminist psycho-social theories reproduce a patriarchal horror of enraged women? Perhaps not deliberately, but the result may be the same. As a political movement, feminism has encouraged women to acknowledge and use their rage, not exclusively (though in part) for instrumental purposes, but toward a larger project of claiming knowledge and identity. Women's therapeutic practice, and its associated literature, certainly validates women's experience of being denied hate and rage. Yet the feminist theories that merge sophisticated psychologies with astute social critique tend to neglect this aspect of women's humanness. This is to say that women's greater sensitivity,

care, empathy, or proclivity for connection are not only socially acceptable; they are also theoretically legitimated.

It is obvious that developing social and political theory that is relational (communitarianism) rather than atomistic (liberalism) is not
enough. Relational political thought, like relational psychology, remains
capable of ignoring aspects of human development and identity that are
crucial to the creation and perpetuation of communities. Theorists cannot afford to deny any aspects of human being that are implicated in the
constitution of groups and ideologies. Feminists know this and have
assumed the burden of reconceptualizing social and political theory to
take account of gender, race, ethnicity, and class. Now the task facing
feminist psycho-social theory is to confront the remaining, and undeni-
ably tenacious, barriers to theorizing the role of all the passions, in
theory and in social life.

Notes

Introduction

1. Slight shadings of meaning are significant in naming such a category. One viable alternative might be, for example, Alison Jaggar's naming of certain emotions as "outlaw" emotions, except that this usage adequately represents more of the social, and less of the psychological, dimension than is sought here. See Jaggar, "Love and Knowledge," 160–62.
2. Baier, "Hume, the Women's Moral Theorist?"
3. Hume, *Moral and Political Philosophy*, 236.
4. The common use of this term is not indicative of agreement on a definition of "object relations." See chapter 2.

1. The Passions and Theories of Community

1. This characterization may appear to apply more to women than to men. However, although they often are less explicitly concerned with males, feminist psycho-social theorists would understand men as exhibiting different (sometimes tragic or dangerous) forms of connection or as struggling to escape connection. As one theorist puts it, "To be independent or separate from others and to create distance from others are both modes of relating." Rachel T. Hare-Mustin, "Autonomy and Gender," 206.
2. Gilligan, "Remapping the Moral Domain, 16.
3. Volkan, *The Need to Have Enemies and Allies*.
4. Sennett, *Authority*.
5. Edelman, *Constructing the Political Spectacle*, 72.
6. Dietz, "Citizenship with a Feminist Face," 32.
7. Tronto, "Beyond Gender Difference to a Theory of Care."
8. MacKinnon, "Feminist Discourse, Moral Values, and the Law," 27.
9. See, e.g., Westkott, "Female Rationality."

10. Aristotle, *Ethics,* 100.

11. Ibid., 127–28.

12. Ibid., 207.

13. An additional, and by no means minor, issue concerns the accuracy of the communitarian versions of the self in liberalism. For discussions see Kymlicka, "Liberalism and Communitarianism," and Wallach, "Liberals, Communitarians, and the Tasks of Political Theory."

14. Walzer, "The Communitarian Critique of Liberalism," 10.

15. Ibid., 21.

16. Simpson, "Moral Conservatism," 38.

17. Ibid., 48.

18. One anomalous work is Unger, *Passion.*

19. Rawls attempts to dissociate himself from an account of the self such as that embodied in this term in "Justice as Fairness: Political Not Metaphysical."

20. Sandel, *Liberalism and the Limits of Justice,* 53.

21. Ibid., 150.

22. Friedman, "Feminism and Modern Friendship."

23. Sandel, *Liberalism and the Limits of Justice,* 153.

24. The distinction between two kinds of subjects, the "simple weigher" and the "strong evaluator," is drawn from Charles Taylor. In his, "What Is Human Agency?" Taylor argues that an orthodox psychoanalytic conception of the self as a locus of drives does not adequately capture the potential for self-reflection. This is a valid criticism.

25. Taylor, "What Is Human Agency?" 130.

26. MacIntyre, *After Virtue,* 204–5.

27. Ibid., 222–26.

28. Okin, *Justice, Gender, and the Family,* 56.

29. Hughes, "The Philosopher's Child," 72.

30. Ibid., 77, emphasis added.

31. Code, "Experience, Knowledge, and Responsibility," 198.

32. MacIntyre, *After Virtue,* 153.

33. This is not a charge reserved for communitarian thought. As indicated in chapter 4, Chodorow criticizes certain radical psychoanalytic-social theories on this score. For Pateman's argument that women's subordination is at the heart of liberal contract theories, see *The Sexual Contract.*

34. Okin, *Justice, Gender, and the Family,* 15, also briefly alludes to certain shared ideas, but with disapprobation.

35. Phelan, *Identity Politics,* 145–46.

36. Opotow, "Moral Exclusion and Injustice: An Introduction," 1, emphasis in the original. For an excellent guide to this literature see Opotow, ed., the special issue of *Journal of Social Issues* entitled *Moral Exclusion and Injustice.*

37. Friedman, "Feminism and Modern Friendship," 151.

38. Ibid., 148.

39. Alford, *The Self in Social Theory,* 9.

40. Sandel, *Liberalism and the Limits of Justice,* 33.

41. This last characterization is not identical with, but is consistent with, the moral psychology of Lawrence Kohlberg. See, e.g., Kohlberg, "From Is to Ought," in which Kohlberg inscribes a normative liberal philosophical perspective in the highest level of moral reasoning.

2. Coming to Terms with the Passions

1. Frye, *Politics of Reality*, 84.
2. For excellent discussions of this translation of proscribed expressiveness into the diagnosis of "madness" see, for example, Chesler, *Women and Madness*, and Showalter, *The Female Malady*.
3. Kramarae and Treichler, *A Feminist Dictionary*.
4. Lorde, *Sister/Outsider*, 124.
5. Ibid., 127.
6. Ibid., 131.
7. Ibid., 128.
8. Ibid., 130.
9. Ibid.
10. Dworkin, "Pornography and Grief," 286.
11. Craib, *Psychoanalysis and Social Theory*, 139.
12. The category of "Kleinians" is a fluid one and, largely, a matter of self-definition. Among the best known Kleinians are Wilfred Bion, Hanna Segal, Donald Meltzer, Isabel Menzies Lyth, and Elizabeth Spillius. Winnicott is treated in this analysis as a Kleinian, even though he led a compromise ("B") group within the British Psychoanalytic Society that avoided loyalty to either Klein or Anna Freud. Winnicott was influenced greatly by Klein even when they disagreed. See Grosskurth, *Melanie Klein*, and Phillips, *Winnicott*, for elaboration.
13. Hinshelwood, *A Dictionary of Kleinian Thought*, 322.
14. The spelling of "phantasy" is deliberate and is the preferred method among Kleinian thinkers of denoting a shift from Freudian to Kleinian theory. For followers of Klein, phantasy is a ubiquitous aspect of mental life, not merely the substitute for reality that thinkers in competing psychoanalytic traditions would make it. See ibid., 32–46.
15. Hinshelwood (ibid., 68) defines "object" as "an unconscious experience or phantasy of a concrete object" within the self.
16. See, e.g., Schafer, *A New Language for Psychoanalysis*.
17. Greenberg and Mitchell, *Object Relations in Psychoanalytic Theory*, 120–21.
18. Ogden, "The Concept of Internal Object Relations," 227.
19. Scholars who have employed object relations theory in this manner to study social systems and phenomena include: Lyth, *Containing Anxiety* and *Dynamics of the Social*, and Jacques "Social Systems as Defence."
20. Alford, *Melanie Klein*, 52.
21. Ibid., 55.
22. Meltzer, "Kleinian Expansion," 178.

23. Bart, "Review," 152, emphasis in the original.
24. Ruddick, *Maternal Thinking*, 268.
25. Gardiner, "Self-Psychology," 772.
26. Gilligan, Brown, and Rogers, "Psyche Embedded," 91.
27. Ruddick, *Maternal Thinking*, 268.
28. Fee, "Critiques of Modern Science," 49.
29. Spelman, *Inessential Woman*, 80–113.
30. Grimshaw, *Philosophy and Feminist Thinking*, 69–70.
31. Flax, "Political Philosophy," 250.
32. Hare-Mustin, "The Gender Dichotomy," 264.
33. Kahn, "Excavating Those Dim Minoan Regions," 33.
34. See, e.g., Ruddick, *Maternal Thinking*, and Young, "Is Male Gender Identity the Cause of Male Domination?" Pateman, *The Sexual Contract*, 33–34, and MacKinnon, *Feminism Unmodified*, 53, make a similar point when they argue that female mothering cannot explain the origins of patriarchy but is rather a consequence of patriarchal forms of dominance.
35. Gardiner, "Self-Psychology," 774.
36. Rossi, "Alice S. Rossi," 496.
37. Chodorow, "Reply," 511.
38. Perry, book reviews, 599.
39. Flax, *Thinking Fragments*, 111.
40. Montefiore, book reviews, 311.
41. See, e.g., Eichenbaum and Orbach, *Understanding Women*, 31–32.
42. See Hughes, *Reshaping the Psychoanalytic Domain*. Chapter 3 contains a discussion of the ways in which Klein overstated, and perhaps misunderstood, the continuity of her thought on the instincts with that of Freud.
43. Alford, *Melanie Klein*.
44. Greenberg and Mitchell, *Object Relations in Psychoanalytic Theory*, 146.
45. Mitchell, *The Selected Melanie Klein*, 19.
46. The following quote, addressed directly to mothers, is an example: "If you do handle your baby well I want you to be able to know that you are doing something of importance." Winnicott, *Babies and Their Mothers*, 18–19.
47. Winnicott, quoted in Hughes, *Reshaping the Psychoanalytic Domain*, 174.
48. Adam Phillips alludes briefly to the contribution of British School theories to the post–World War II construction of a pervasive ideology of women's nurturance and responsibility for family life in *Winnicott*, 9–10.
49. Winnicott, *The Maturational Processes*, 176.
50. Winnicott, *Playing and Reality*, 70.
51. Phillips, *Winnicott*, 111.
52. Keller, *Reflections on Gender and Science*.
53. Sayers, "Melanie Klein."
54. Sayers, *Sexual Contradictions*.
55. In her 1991 book, *Mothers of Psychoanalysis*, Sayers does imply that Klein is an object relations theorist (one chapter on Klein is entitled "Object Relations"), but the point is not pursued explicitly.

56. Chodorow, *Feminism and Psychoanalytic Theory*, 148–53.
57. Mahler, Pine, and Bergman, *The Psychological Birth of the Human Infant*.
58. Two noteworthy exceptions to this generalization are: Dinnerstein, *The Mermaid and the Minotaur*, and Chernin, *The Hungry Self*. See also the responses to Klein in the Summer 1990 issue of *Women: A Cultural Review*.
59. See, e.g., Hughes, *Reshaping the Psychoanalytic Domain*, and Greenberg and Mitchell, *Object Relations in Psychoanalytic Theory*.
60. "Aggression" has been associated with so many conceptual difficulties that many theorists have suggested abandoning it altogether; see Harré and Lamb for a review of some of these issues within psychology. They note in *The Dictionary of Personality and Social Psychology*, 8, that "aggression might be viewed as a motivational state, a personality characteristic, a socially learned role requirement." This definitional problem notwithstanding, many, and perhaps most, psychoanalytic theorists have found it useful to employ the term to describe not just observable and measurable violent behaviors but a range of "internal motivational state[s]."
61. Sayers, "Melanie Klein," 31.
62. Sayers, "Feminism and Mothering," 238.
63. See especially Sayers, "Melanie Klein."
64. Ibid., 32–36.
65. This particular criticism as it applies to Dinnerstein is difficult to fathom given Dinnerstein's account of rage in the relations between mothers and children (especially mothers and daughters). For a different perspective see chapter 5.
66. Flax, "Conflict between Nurturance and Autonomy," 61.
67. Flax, "Postmodernism and Gender Relations," 641.
68. Moi, "Patriarchal Thought," 191.
69. Ibid., 204.

3. *The Voices of Care and Reparation*

1. Gilligan has, however differently than other developmental psychologists, constructed a stage theory. This point has been overlooked by many commentators, although others have criticized particulars of Gilligan's version of stages.
2. Gilligan, *In a Different Voice*, 74.
3. Gilligan, "Preface." As this suggests, Gilligan appears to abandon the assumption of an invariant sequence of developmental stages in women's moral response.
4. Flanagan and Jackson, in "Justice, Care, and Gender," characterize Gilligan's version of selfhood in these terms. See also Sandel, *Liberalism and the Limits of Justice*, for a more extensive use of the categories of "thinness" and "thickness" in his criticism of Rawlsian theory.
5. The characterization is that of Hayles in "Anger in Different Voices."
6. This category of criticism has been made both by feminists, such as Ben-

habib in "The Generalized and the Concrete Other," and nonfeminists, such as Sullivan in "A Study of Kohlberg's Structural Theory."

7. Benhabib, "The Generalized and the Concrete Other," 176. Benhabib is less critical of Gilligan in spite of Gilligan's ostensible situation within the same paradigm.

8. See Kohlberg, "From Is to Ought," and Schott, *Cognition and Eros.*

9. Gilligan, "Do the Social Sciences Have an Adequate Theory of Moral Development?" 45.

10. Gilligan, *In a Different Voice,* 2.

11. Gilligan, "Woman's Place in Man's Life Cycle," 68.

12. Gilligan, "Reply by Carol Gilligan," in Kerber et al., "On *In a Different Voice,*" 326.

13. This argument is made most forcefully in Gilligan, "The Origins of Morality."

14. Gilligan, "The Conquistador," 76.

15. The phrase is originally drawn from Murdoch's *Sovereignty of Good.*

16. Gilligan, "The Conquistador," 77.

17. Gilligan, "Exit-Voice Dilemmas," 151.

18. Broughton, "Women's Rationality and Men's Virtues," 633.

19. Young, "Impartiality and the Civic Public," 58–59.

20. Benhabib, "The Generalized and the Concrete Other," 87.

21. Ibid., 176.

22. See, e.g., Auerbach et al., "Commentary."

23. Haste, "Why Thinking about Feeling Isn't the Same as Feeling about Feeling," 218, emphasis in the original.

24. Ibid.

25. Both Flanagan, "Virtue, Sex, and Gender," and Nails, "Social-Scientific Sexisms," criticize Gilligan for only measuring and interpreting the cognitive skills of her subjects. Their criticism is as problematic as Haste's defense of Gilligan.

26. Gilligan, *In a Different Voice,* 22.

27. Code, "Experience, Knowledge, and Responsibility," 196.

28. Gilligan, "Reply by Carol Gilligan," in Kerber et al., "On *In a Different Voice,*" 328.

29. Greeno and Maccoby, "How Different Is the 'Different Voice'?"

30. Luria, "A Methodological Critique," 319.

31. Stack, "The Culture of Gender: Women and Men of Color," 323. For Gilligan's reply to criticisms based on the issue of race, see Gilligan and Attanucci, "Two Moral Orientations," 83.

32. See, e.g., MacKinnon, *Feminism Unmodified,* 38–39. For a response to this charge in support of Gilligan, see Meyers, "The Socialized Individual and Individual Autonomy." For a related critique that is not explicitly linked to Gilligan's work, see Tronto, "Women and Caring."

33. See, e.g., Grimshaw, *Philosophy and Feminist Thinking.*

34. Luria, "A Methodological Critique," 320.

35. Baier, "Hume, the Women's Moral Theorist?" 48. However, Baier simultaneously understands Gilligan's work as addressing the role of the "passions" in moral development.
36. Broughton, "Women's Rationality and Men's Virtues," 633.
37. See also Sayers, "Freud Revisited," for a suggestion of the possibility that Gilligan's subjects shape their responses to accord with the researchers' expectations.
38. Hayles, "Anger in Different Voices," 23.
39. Gilligan, *In a Different Voice*, 138.
40. Hayles, "Anger in Different Voices," 30.
41. Sayers, "Freud Revisited," 203.
42. Gilligan, "Changing the Questions," 208.
43. Gilligan, *In a Different Voice*, 93.
44. Gilligan, "Changing the Questions," 208.
45. Greeno and Maccoby, "How Different Is the 'Different Voice'?" characterize Gilligan's contribution in this way.
46. Gilligan, *In a Different Voice*, 45.
47. Pollack and Gilligan, "Images of Violence."
48. Ibid., 160.
49. The results of these experiments, and hence Gilligan's conclusions, have been challenged by Benton et al., "Is Hostility Linked with Affiliation?"
50. Gilligan, "Preface," 20–21.
51. Gilligan, *In a Different Voice*, 124.
52. Gilligan, "New Maps of Development," 211.
53. Freud, quoted in Gilligan, *In a Different Voice*, 7.
54. Ibid., 23.
55. Freud, *Civilization and Its Discontents*.
56. Gilligan, "Moral Orientation," 28.
57. Gilligan, "Do the Social Sciences Have an Adequate Theory of Moral Development," 48. Gilligan argues that she wishes not to depose the "justice perspective" on morality, only to furnish its complementary perspective. Both together reveal the "dialectic," something that neither can do alone.
58. Williams, *Problems of the Self*, 222–23.
59. Sagan, *Freud, Women, and Morality*, 126.
60. Alford, *Melanie Klein*, 4–5.
61. Meltzer, *The Kleinian Development*, 9.
62. Ibid., 10–11.
63. In Klein's thought, the paranoid-schizoid position precedes the depressive position; its successful negotiation is a necessary condition for passage into the depressive position. However, Winnicott spoke to the relation between the positions in development in this way: "Integration of a personality does not arrive at a certain time on a certain day. It comes and goes, and even when well attained it can be lost through unfortunate environmental chance." Winnicott, *Collected Papers*, 205.
64. Segal, *Introduction*, 68.

65. Klein, *Writings*, vol. 1, 342.
66. Greenberg and Mitchell, *Object Relations in Psychoanalytic Theory*, 126.
67. Winnicott often describes this "love" not as ruth-less, but as the natural consequence of a "pre-ruth era." By this he means that the capacity for pity and remorse are not yet present and that there is no intention to do harm. See, e.g., *Collected Papers*, 210–11.
68. Winnicott, *Collected Papers*, 199–201. This critical process of personal "real-making," as well as the process of "destruction" whereby others are made real, is discussed in analyzing the social theory of Jessica Benjamin in chapter 4.
69. Winnicott, *The Maturational Processes*, 176.
70. Ibid.
71. Ibid., 81.
72. Ibid., 25.
73. Silverman, "Female Bonding," 213, suggests that Gilligan's findings on the "affiliative concerns" of women are consistent with Klein's clinical discovery of a superego in women that is "occupied" with "reparative strivings," but she does not elaborate on this consistency.
74. Gilligan, "The Origins of Morality," 120.
75. Klein, *Writings*, vol. 1, 313.
76. See, e.g., Gilligan, Brown, and Rogers, "Psyche Embedded," and Gilligan, "New Maps of Development."

4. The Passions in Feminist Object Relations

1. Chodorow, *The Reproduction of Mothering*. In the introduction to the more recent *Feminism and Psychoanalytic Theory*, Chodorow softens this distinction, merely noting that object relations theory "emerged" from the work of Klein.
2. Chodorow, *The Reproduction of Mothering*, 95, credits Jeanne Lampl-de Groot, rather than Klein, with the "discovery" of—and thus, presumably, with much of the subsequent clinical and theoretical emphasis on—preoedipal relations.
3. Ibid., 167.
4. A thorough exposition of "sex-role socialization" in males is found in "Being and Doing," in Chodorow, *Feminism and Psychoanalytic Theory*, 23–24. Although the method in this 1971 essay is not psychoanalytic, little of Chodorow's analysis of male development is altered by her later turn to psychoanalytic theory. The early arguments are consistent with her assertions in *The Reproduction of Mothering*, e.g., 167, that the internal object world of women is more "complex" than than of men.
5. Chodorow, *The Reproduction of Mothering*, 7.
6. Chodorow characterizes her work in this way; see, e.g., "Beyond Drive Theory," in Chodorow, *Feminism and Psychoanalytic Theory*, 114–53.
7. Chodorow, *The Reproduction of Mothering*, 42–50.

8. Moi, "Patriarchal Thought," 191.

9. Chodorow, *The Reproduction of Mothering*, 51.

10. Nancy Chodorow and Susan Contratto, "The Fantasy of the Perfect Mother," in Chodorow, *Feminism and Psychoanalytic Theory*, 79–96.

11. Thus, Chodorow suggests that the acquisition of an "unproblematic sense of self" is partially a function of the absence—both in care giver and child—of processes like projection.

12. Chodorow and Contratto, "The Fantasy of the Perfect Mother," 89.

13. Chodorow, *Feminism and Psychoanalytic Theory*, 154–62.

14. Sometimes when Chodorow addresses herself to this problem, she writes of "women" and sometimes of "mothers." Chodorow has been accused of collapsing the categories of "mother" and "woman" in a way that leaves unchallenged and unreformed the patriarchal identity between the two. To the degree that Chodorow fails to incorporate divergences from and resistances to this identity as, for example, in her neglect of lesbian identity, this is certainly a legitimate criticism. However, it is clear that part of what she wants to critique is the unexamined merging of "mother" and "woman" that she finds corroborated by fantasy, cultural representations, and theories (even those of feminists like Dorothy Dinnerstein).

15. Chodorow and Contratto, "The Fantasy of the Perfect Mother," 83.

16. Chodorow, *Feminism and Psychoanalytic Theory*, 114–53.

17. Marcuse, *Eros and Civilization*.

18. Brown, *Life against Death*.

19. Chodorow and Contratto, "The Fantasy of the Perfect Mother," 95.

20. In *Feminism and Psychoanalytic Theory*, 114–53, Chodorow suggests that Winnicott's concept of "transitional space" can provide a way to understand intersubjectivity. For a critical perspective, see the discussion of Winnicott and Benjamin below.

21. Chodorow, *The Reproduction of Mothering*, 65.

22. "A particular unconscious process, affect, or structural form can express itself in almost endless behavioral as well as conscious psychological modes." Ibid., 41.

23. Ibid., 83.

24. Ibid., 80.

25. Ibid., 97.

26. Ibid., 70.

27. What is at issue in this statement is not the question of whether biological mothers, or women in general, *should* provide perfect care for children but whether the mismatching of the child's true needs to adult provision is the primary cause of disagreeable passions.

28. Craib, *Psychoanalysis and Social Theory*, 140.

29. Klein, *Writings*, vol. 1, 309.

30. Bion, "Attacks on Linking," 96–99. Bion was an analyst and theorist of groups whose thought is significantly indebted to Kleinian theory. See Hinshelwood, *A Dictionary of Kleinian Thought*, for a review of litera-

ture and the characterization of Bion as the most "original" of post-Kleinian thinkers.

31. Klein, *Writings*, vol. 1, 327.
32. See, e.g., ibid., 329.
33. Of course, feminist theorists do tend to note this dynamic, especially in masculine development. Perhaps because of this equation with "radical" individuation, it is virtually always regarded as dysfunctional and undesirable.
34. Riviere, "Hate, Greed, and Aggression," 42.
35. Phillips, *Winnicott*, 132.
36. Chodorow, *Feminism and Psychoanalytic Theory*, 156.
37. Riviere, quoted in ibid., *Feminism and Psychoanalytic Theory*, 158.
38. Chodorow, *The Reproduction of Mothering*, 33.
39. Chodorow, *Feminism and Psychoanalytic Theory*, 3.
40. Benjamin, "The Bonds of Love," 148.
41. This is true even though Benjamin sometimes qualifies the perfect gender symmetry presumed by much of her theory (e.g., "But the slave of love is not always a woman or only a heterosexual," ibid., 144).
42. Ibid.
43. Ibid., 150.
44. Benjamin, *The Bonds of Love*, 33.
45. Ibid., 36.
46. Ibid., 35.
47. Ibid., 36.
48. Benjamin, "The Bonds of Love," 165.
49. Ibid. Lest the terms *sadist* and *masochist* evoke confusion, Benjamin states that she does not use these to connote only the partners in consensual sexual violence. She uses these terms, instead, to describe erotic domination in "normal love."
50. One passage is not consistent with this general conclusion. Benjamin states in writing of the failure of recognition, "We see how the search for recognition can become a power struggle: how assertion becomes aggression." *The Bonds of Love*, 28. Here "aggression" and the "rage" of other passages are made more nearly synonymous, but this usage is anomalous.
51. Ibid., 214.
52. Benjamin, "Master and Slave," 291.
53. Benjamin, *The Bonds of Love*, 20–21.
54. Ibid., 21.
55. Ibid., 39.
56. Ibid., 21, emphasis in the original.
57. Winnicott, quoted in ibid., 38, emphasis in the original.
58. Ibid., 69.
59. Ibid., 71.
60. Ibid., 73.
61. Ibid., 38.

62. Sayers, *Sexual Contradictions,* 67, reads Winnicott in this way and criticizes him on this score: "In effect, unlike Klein, Winnicott treats the child's internal world as a reflection of an essentially uncontradictory external world."
63. Craib, *Psychoanalysis and Social Theory,* 166.
64. Winnicott, *Playing and Reality,* 2. The discussion of the concept of transitional space is drawn largely from Winnicott's essays in this collection.
65. Ibid., 90, emphasis added.
66. Ibid., 11.

5. Reconstituting the Self in Social Theory

1. For an exposition of this theme in liberal political thought, see especially Hirschman, *The Passions and the Interests.*
2. Ruddick, *Maternal Thinking,* 82.
3. Miller, *The Drama of the Gifted Child,* 9.
4. Dinnerstein, *The Mermaid and the Minotaur,* 4.
5. Ibid., 77.
6. Ibid., 166.
7. Dinnerstein uses the singular form in this way to connote the infantile resonance of the perception of mother (and, then, more generally of women), not to suggest an ahistorical and undifferentiated category, as such a term might be used.
8. The use of the notion of life and death drives, eros and thanatos, can be found particularly in Dinnerstein, "Afterword."
9. Sayers, book reviews, 260.
10. Dinnerstein, *The Mermaid and the Minotaur,* xiii.
11. Ibid., 95.
12. Ibid., 5.
13. Ibid., 237.
14. Ibid., 30.
15. Whereas for Klein the course of envy is to some extent determined by "constitutional" (innate) factors, Dinnerstein rejects a biological argument. Moreover, Dinnerstein takes as metaphoric and symbolic the more concrete elements of Klein's theory (i.e., the "good breast") and ignores much of Klein's extrapolation of infantile experience (ibid., 96). These are not uncommon strategies of interpretation among present scholars.
16. Klein, *Writings,* vol. 3, 180, 189.
17. Ibid., 181.
18. Ibid., 189.
19. Dinnerstein, *The Mermaid and the Minotaur,* 95.
20. Alford, *Melanie Klein.*
21. Dinnerstein, *The Mermaid and the Minotaur,* 102.
22. Fanon, *Black Skin, White Masks.*
23. Spillius, "Some Developments from the Work of Melanie Klein," 331–32.

24. Bion, "Attacks on Linking," 95, presumes that it is part of "the foundation on which normal development rests."
25. Dinnerstein, The Mermaid and the Minotaur, 88–89.
26. Benjamin, The Bonds of Love, 265.
27. Flax, Thinking Fragments, 164.
28. Segal, "Some Clinical Implications of Melanie Klein's Work," 269.
29. Sayers, Sexual Contradictions, 62–63.
30. Lifton, The Broken Connection, 50.
31. Grosskurth, Melanie Klein, 233.
32. Alford, The Self in Social Theory, 11.
33. For a subtle exploration of Kernberg's position among object relational models see Greenberg and Mitchell, Object Relations in Psychoanalytic Theory, chapter 10. Their discussion links Kernberg with Klein. They suggest that Kernberg's is a theory of affect and interpersonal experience, and they deemphasize the drive aspects of his theory in much the same way that other commentators have interpreted Klein.
34. For further discussion and elaboration of Volkan's extension of object relations theory into international relations see Volkan, Julius, and Montville, The Psychodynamics of International Relationships.
35. Alford, Melanie Klein, 11.

Bibliography

Alford, C. Fred. 1989. *Melanie Klein and critical social theory: An account of art, reason and politics based on her psychoanalytic theory*. New Haven: Yale University Press.

————. 1991. *The self in social theory*. New Haven: Yale University Press.

Aristotle. 1969. *The ethics of Aristotle*. Translated by J. A. K. Thompson. Baltimore: Penguin.

Auerbach, Judy, Linda Blum, Vicki Smith, and Christine Williams. 1985. Commentary: On Gilligan's *In a Different Voice*. *Feminist Studies* 11(1):149–61.

Baier, Annette C. 1987. Hume, the women's moral theorist? In *Women and moral theory*, edited by Eva Feder Kittay and Diana T. Meyers, 37–55. Savage, Md.: Rowman and Littlefield.

Balint, Michael. 1968. *The basic fault: Therapeutic aspects of regression*. London: Tavistock.

Bart, Pauline. 1983. Review of Chodorow's, *The reproduction of mothering*. In *Mothering: Essays in feminist theory*, edited by Joyce Trebilcot, 147–52. Savage, Md.: Rowman and Littlefield.

Benhabib, Seyla. 1987. The generalized and the concrete other: The Kohlberg-Gilligan controversy and feminist theory. In *Feminism as critique: On the politics of gender*, edited by Seyla Benhabib and Drucilla Cornell, 77–181. Minneapolis: University of Minnesota Press.

Benjamin, Jessica. 1988. *The bonds of love: Psychoanalysis, feminism and the problem of domination*. New York: Pantheon.

————. 1980. The bonds of love: Rational violence and erotic domination. *Feminist Studies* 6(1):144–74.

————. Master and slave: The fantasy of erotic domination. In *Powers of desire: The politics of sexuality*, edited by Ann Snitow, 280–99. New York: Monthly Review Press.

Benton, Cynthia J., Anthony C. R. Hernandez, Adeny Schmidt, Mary D.

Schmitz, Anna J. Stone, and Bernard Weiner. 1983. Is hostility linked with affiliation among males and with achievement among females? A critique of Pollack and Gilligan. *Journal of Personality and Social Psychology* 45(5):1167–71.

Bion, Wilfred. 1988. Attacks on linking. In *Melanie Klein today: Developments in theory and practice*, edited by Elizabeth Bott Spillius. Vol. 1, *Mainly theory*, 87–101. New York: Routledge.

Broughton, John M. 1983. Women's rationality and men's virtues: A critique of gender dualism in Gilligan's theory of moral development. *Social Research* 50(3):597–642.

Brown, Norman O. 1959. *Life against death.* New York: Vintage.

Chernin, Kim. 1985. *The hungry self: Women, eating, and identity.* New York: Times Books.

Chesler, Phyllis. 1972. *Women and madness.* New York: Avon.

Chodorow, Nancy. 1979. Feminism and difference: Gender, relation, and difference in psychoanalytic perspective. *Socialist Review* 9(4):51–69.

———. 1989. *Feminism and psychoanalytic theory.* New Haven: Yale University Press.

———. 1981. Reply by Nancy Chodorow. In Judith Lorber, Rose Laub Coser, Alice S. Rossi, and Nancy Chodorow, On *The reproduction of mothering: A methodological debate. Signs* 6(3):500–514.

———. 1978. *The reproduction of mothering: Psychoanalysis and the sociology of gender.* Berkeley: University of California Press.

Code, Lorraine. 1988. Experience, knowledge, and responsibility. In *Feminist perspectives in philosophy*, edited by Morwenna Griffiths and Margaret Whitford, 187–204. Indianapolis: Indiana University Press.

Craib, Ian. 1990. *Psychoanalysis and social theory: The limits of sociology.* Amherst: University of Massachusetts Press.

Dietz, Mary G. 1985. Citizenship with a feminist face: The problem with maternal thinking. *Political Theory* 13(1):19–37.

Dinnerstein, Dorothy. 1983. Afterword: Toward the mobilization of Eros. In *Face to face: Fathers, mothers, masters, monsters—Essays for a nonsexist future*, edited by Meg Murray McGavron, 293–310. Westport, Conn.: Greenwood Press.

———. 1976. *The mermaid and the minotaur: Sexual arrangements and human malaise.* New York: Harper and Row.

Dworkin, Andrea. 1987. *Intercourse.* New York: Free Press.

———. 1980. Pornography and grief. In *Take back the night: Women on pornography*, edited by Laura Lederer, 286–91. New York: Morrow.

Edelman, Murray. 1988. *Constructing the political spectacle.* Chicago: University of Chicago Press.

Eichenbaum, Luise, and Susie Orbach. 1983. *Understanding women: A feminist psychoanalytic approach.* New York: Basic Books.

Fanon, Frantz. 1967. *Black skin, white masks.* Translated by Charles Lam Markmann. New York: Grove.

Fee, Elizabeth. 1986. Critiques of modern science: The relationship of feminism to other radical epistemologies. In *Feminist approaches to science,* edited by Ruth Blier, 42–56. New York: Pergamon.

Flanagan, Owen. 1982. Virtue, sex, and gender: Some philosophical reflections on the moral psychology debate. *Ethics* 92(3):499–512.

Flanagan, Owen, and Kathryn Jackson. 1987. Justice, care, and gender: The Kohlberg-Gilligan debate revisited. *Ethics* 97(3):622–37.

Flax, Jane. 1981. The conflict between nurturance and autonomy in mother-daughter relationships and within feminism. In *Women and mental health,* edited by Elizabeth Howell and Marjorie Bayes, 51–69. New York: Basic Books.

———. 1983. Political philosophy and the patriarchal unconscious: A psychoanalytic perspective on epistemology and metaphysics. In *Discovering reality: Feminist perspectives on epistemology, metaphysics, and philosophy of science,* edited by Sandra Harding and Merrill B. Hintikka, 245–81. Boston: D. Reidel.

———. 1987. Postmodernism and gender relations in feminist theory. *Signs* 12(4):621–43.

———. 1990. *Thinking fragments: Psychoanalysis, feminism, and post-modernism in the contemporary west.* Berkeley: University of California Press.

Freud, Sigmund. 1961. *Civilization and its discontents.* Translated by James Strachey. New York: Norton.

Friedman, Marilyn. 1990. Feminism and modern friendship: Dislocating the community. In *Feminism and Political Theory,* edited by Cass Sunstein, 143–58. Chicago: University of Chicago Press.

Frye, Marilyn. 1983. *The politics of reality: Essays in feminist theory.* Trumansburg, N.Y.: Crossing Press.

Gardiner, Judith Kegan. 1987. Self-psychology as feminist theory. *Signs* 12(4):761–80.

Gilligan, Carol. 1987. Changing the questions: A reply to Philibert and Sayers. *New Ideas in Psychology* 5(2):207–8.

———. 1984. The conquistador and the dark continent: Reflections on the psychology of love. *Daedalus* 113:75–95.

———. 1983. Do the social sciences have an adequate theory of moral development? In *Social science as moral inquiry,* edited by Norma Haan, Robert N. Bellah, Paul Rabinow, and William M. Sullivan, 33–51. New York: Columbia University Press.

———. 1988. Exit-voice dilemmas in adolescent development. In *Mapping the moral domain,* edited by Carol Gilligan, Janie Victoria Ward, and Jill McLean Taylor, 141–58. Cambridge: Harvard University Press.

———. 1982. *In a different voice: Psychological theory and women's development.* Cambridge: Harvard University Press.

———. 1987. Moral orientation and moral development. In *Women and moral theory,* edited by Eva Feder Kittay and Diana T. Meyers, 19–33. Savage, Md.: Rowman and Littlefield.

————. 1982. New maps of development: New visions of maturity. *American Journal of Orthopsychiatry* 52(2):199–212.

————. 1990. Preface. In *Making connections: The relational worlds of adolescent girls at Emma Willard School*, edited by Carol Gilligan, Nona P. Lyons, and Trudy J. Hanmer, 6–29. Cambridge: Harvard University Press.

————. 1988. Remapping the moral domain: New images of the self in relationship. In *Mapping the moral domain*, edited by Carol Gilligan, Janie Victoria Ward, and Jill McLean Taylor, 3–20. Cambridge: Harvard University Press.

————. 1987. Woman's place in man's life cycle. In *Feminism and methodology: Social science issues*, edited by Sandra Harding, 57–73. Bloomington: Indiana University Press.

Gilligan, Carol, and Jane Attanucci. 1988. Two moral orientations: Gender differences and similarities. In *Mapping the moral domain*, edited by Carol Gilligan, Janie Victoria Ward, Jill McLean Taylor, 73–86. Cambridge: Harvard University Press.

Gilligan, Carol, Lyn Brown, and Annie Rogers. 1990. Psyche embedded: A place for body, relationships, and culture in personality theory. In *Studing persons and lives*, edited by A. I. Rabin, Robert A. Zucker, Robert A. Emmons, and Susan Frank, 86–147. New York: Springer.

Gilligan, Carol, and Susan Pollack. 1988. The vulnerable and invulnerable physician. In *Mapping the moral domain*, edited by Carol Gilligan, Janie Victoria Ward, and Jill McLean Taylor, 245–62. Cambridge: Harvard University Press.

Gilligan, Carol, and Grant Wiggins. 1988. The origins of morality in early childhood relationships. In *Mapping the moral domain*, edited by Carol Gilligan, Janie Victoria Ward, and Jill McLean Taylor, 111–38. Cambridge: Harvard University Press.

Greenberg, Jay R., and Stephen A. Mitchell. 1983. *Object relations in psychoanalytic theory*. Cambridge: Harvard University Press.

Greeno, Catherine, and Eleanor E. Maccoby. 1986. How different is the "different voice"? In Linda K. Kerber et al., On *In a different voice*: An interdisciplinary forum. *Signs* 11(2):310–16.

Grimshaw, Jean. 1986. *Philosophy and feminist thinking*. Minneapolis: University of Minnisota Press.

Grosskurth, Phyllis. 1986. *Melanie Klein: Her world and her work*. New York: Knopf.

Gutman, Amy. 1985. Communitarian critics of liberalism. *Philosophy and Public Affairs* 14(3):308–22.

Haraway, Donna. 1990. A manifesto for cyborgs: Science, technology, and socialist feminism in the 1980s. In *Feminism/Postmodernism*, edited by Linda Nicholson, 190–233. New York: Routledge.

Hare-Mustin, Rachel T. 1986. Autonomy and gender: Some questions for therapists. *Psychotherapy* 26(2):205–12.

————. 1987. The gender dichotomy and developmental theory: A response to Sayers. *New Ideas in Psychology* 5(2):262–67.

Harré, Rom, and Roger Lamb. 1986. *The Dictionary of Personality and Social Psychology*. Cambridge: MIT Press.

Haste, Helen. 1987. Why thinking about feeling isn't the same as feeling about feeling, and why post-androgyny is dialectical not regressive: A response to Philibert and Sayers. *New Ideas in Psychology* 5(2):215–21.

Hayles, N. Katherine. 1986. Anger in different voices: Carol Gilligan and *The mill on the Floss*. *Signs* 12(1):23–39.

Hinshelwood, R. D. 1989. *A dictionary of Kleinian thought*. London: Free Association.

Hirschman, Albert O. 1977. *The passions and the interests: Political arguments for capitalism before its triumph*. Princeton, N.J.: Princeton University Press.

Hughes, Judith. 1988. The philosopher's child. In *Feminist perspectives in philosophy*, edited by Morwenna Griffiths and Margaret Whitford, 72–89. Indianapolis: Indiana University Press.

Hughes, Judith M. 1989. *Reshaping the psychoanalytic domain: The work of Melanie Klein, W. R. D. Fairbairn, and D. W. Winnicott*. Berkeley: University of California Press.

Hume, David. 1948. *Moral and political philosophy*. Ed. Henry D. Aiken. New York: Hafner.

Hurston, Zora Neale. 1990. *Their eyes were watching God*. New York: Harper and Row.

Jacques, Elliott. 1955. Social systems as defence against persecutory and depressive anxiety: A contribution to the psycho-analytical study of social systems. In *New directions in psycho-analysis,* edited by Melanie Klein, Paula Heimann, and Roger Money-Kyrle, 478–98. London: Tavistock.

Jaggar, Alison M. 1988. *Feminist politics and human nature*. Totowa, N.J.: Rowman and Littlefield.

————. 1989. Love and knowledge: Emotion in feminist epistemology. In *Gender/body/knowledge: Feminist reconstructions of being and knowing,* edited by Alison M. Jagger and Susan R. Bordo, 145–71. New Brunswick, N.J.: Rutgers University Press.

Kahn, Coppelia. 1982. Excavating those dim Minoan regions: Maternal subtexts in patriarchal literature. *Diacritics* 12:32–41.

Keller, Evelyn Fox. 1985. *Reflections on gender and science*. New Haven: Yale University Press.

Kerber, Linda K., Catherine G. Greeno, Eleanor E. Maccoby, Zella Luria, Carol B. Stack, and Carol Gilligan. 1986. On *In a different voice*: An interdisciplinary forum. *Signs* 11(2):304–33.

Klein, Melanie. 1975. *The writings of Melanie Klein*. Vol. 1, *Love, guilt, and reparation and other works, 1921–1945*. New York: Free Press.

————. 1975. *The writings of Melanie Klein*. Vol. 3, *Envy and gratitude and other works, 1946–1963*. New York: Free Press.

Kohlberg, Lawrence. 1981. From is to ought: How to commit the naturalistic fallacy and get away with it in the study of moral development. In *The philosophy of moral development: Moral stages and the idea of justice*, edited by Lawrence Kohlberg, 101–89. San Francisco: Harper and Row.

Kohlberg, Lawrence, Charles Levine, and Alexandra Hewer. 1984. Synopses and detailed replies to critics. In *The psychology of moral development: The nature and validity of moral stages*, edited by Lawrence Kohlberg, 320–86. San Francisco: Harper and Row.

Kramarae, Cheris, and Paula A. Treichler. 1985. *A Feminist Dictionary*. Boston: Pandora.

Kymlicka, Will. 1988. Liberalism and communitarianism. *Canadian Journal of Philosophy* 18(2):182–204.

Lifton, Robert Jay. 1983. *The broken connection: On death and the continuity of life*. New York: Basic Books.

Lorber, Judith. 1981. In Judith Lorber, Rose Laub Coser, Alice S. Rossi, and Nancy Chodorow. On *The reproduction of mothering*: A methodological debate. *Signs* 6(3):482–514.

Lorde, Audre. 1984. *Sister/Outsider*. Trumansburg, N.Y.: Crossing Press.

Luria, Zella. 1986. A methodological critique. In Linda K. Kerber et al., On *In a different voice*: An interdisciplinary forum. *Signs* 11(2):316–21.

Lyth, Isabel Menzies. 1988. *Containing anxiety in institutions. Selected essays*. Vol. 1. London: Free Association.

———. 1989. *The dynamics of the social. Selected essays*. Vol. 2. London: Free Association.

MacIntyre, Alasdair. 1981. *After virtue: A study in moral theory*. Notre Dame: University of Notre Dame Press.

MacKinnon, Catharine. 1987. *Feminism unmodified: Discourses on life and law*. Cambridge: Harvard University Press.

———. 1985. Feminist discourse, moral values, and the law—A conversation. *Buffalo Law Review* 34:11–87.

Mahler, Margaret, Fred Pine, and Anni Bergman. 1975. *The psychological birth of the human infant: Symbiosis and individuation*. New York: Basic Books.

Mann, Jeff. 1987. Frost fugue. Unpublished poem.

Marcuse, Herbert. 1966. *Eros and civilization: A philosophical inquiry into Freud*. Boston: Beacon.

Markus, Maria. 1989. The "anti-feminism" of Hannah Arendt. In *Hannah Arendt: Thinking, judging, freedom*, edited by Gisela T. Kaplan and Clive Kessler, 119–29. Sydney, Australia: Allen and Unwin.

Meltzer, Donald. 1978. *The Kleinian development*. Pershire, Scotland: Clunie Press.

———. 1981. The Kleinian expansion of Freud's metapsychology. *International Journal of Psycho-Analysis* 62:177–85.

Meyers, Diana T. 1987. The socialized individual and individual autonomy: An intersection between philosophy and psychology. In *Women and moral theory*, edited by Eva Feder Kittay and Diana T. Meyers, 139–53. Savage, Md.: Rowman and Littlefield.

Miller, Alice. 1981. *The Drama of the Gifted Child: The Search for the True Self.* Translated by Ruth Ward. New York: Basic Books.

———. 1983. *For your own good: Hidden cruelty in child-rearing and the roots of violence.* Translated by Hildegarde and Hunter Hannum. New York: Farrar, Straus, and Giroux.

Mitchell, Juliet, ed. 1987. *The selected Melanie Klein.* New York: Free Press.

Moi, Toril. 1989. Patriarchal thought and the drive for knowledge. In *Between feminism and psychoanalysis,* edited by Teresa Brennan, 189–205. New York: Routledge.

Montefiore, Janet. 1990. Book reviews: Nancy Chodorow. *Feminism and psychoanalytic theory;* Teresa Brennan, ed. *Between feminism and psychonanalysis. Women: A cultural review* 1(3):308–13.

Murdoch, Iris. 1971. *The sovereignty of good.* New York: Schocken.

Nails, Debra. 1983. Social-scientific sexisms: Gilligan's mismeasure of man. *Social Research* 50(3):643–64.

Ogden, Thomas H. 1983. The concept of internal object relations. *International Journal of Psycho-Analysis* 64(2):227–41.

Okin, Susan Moller. 1989. *Justice, gender, and the family.* New York: Basic Books.

Opotow, Susan. 1990. Moral exclusion and injustice: An introduction. *Journal of Social Issues* 46(1):1–20.

———, ed. 1990. *Moral exclusion and injustice. Journal of Social Issues.* 46(1).

Pateman, Carole. 1988. *The sexual contract.* Stanford: Stanford University Press.

Perry, Ruth. 1991. Book reviews: *Feminism and psychoanalytic theory, Postmodernism in the contemporary west, Refiguring the father: New feminist readings of patriarchy. Signs* 16(3):597–603.

Phelan, Shane. 1989. *Identity politics: Lesbian feminism and the limits of community.* Philadelphia: Temple University Press.

Phillips, Adam. 1988. *Winnicott.* Cambridge: Harvard University Press.

Piercy, Marge. 1980. *The moon is always female.* New York: Knopf.

Pollack, Susan, and Carol Gilligan. 1982. Images of violence in thematic apperception test stories. *Journal of Personality and Social Psychology* 42(1):159–67.

Rawls, John. 1985. Justice as fairness: Political not metaphysical. *Philosophy and Public Affairs* 14(3):223–51.

———. 1971. *A Theory of Justice.* Cambridge: Harvard University Press.

Riviere, Joan. 1964. Hate, greed, and aggression. In *Love, hate, and reparation,* edited by Melanie Klein and Joan Riviere, 3–53. New York: Norton.

Rossi, Alice S. 1981. Alice S. Rossi. In Judith Lorber, Rose Laub Coser, Alice S. Rossi, and Nancy Chodorow, On *The reproduction of mothering:* A methodological debate. *Signs* 6(3):492–500.

Ruddick, Sara. 1982. Maternal thinking. In *Rethinking the family: Some feminist questions,* edited by Barry Thorne and Marilyn Yalom, 76–94. New York: Longman.

———. 1989. *Maternal thinking: Toward a politics of peace.* Boston: Beacon Press.

Sagan, Eli. 1988. *Freud, women and morality: The psychology of good and evil.* New York: Basic Books.

Sandel, Michael J. 1982. *Liberalism and the limits of justice.* Cambridge: Cambridge University Press.

Sayers, Janet. 1981. Book reviews: *The rocking of the cradle and the ruling of the world; The reproduction of mothering. Women's Studies International Quarterly* 4(1):260–62.

———. 1984. Feminism and mothering: A Kleinian perspective. *Women's Studies International Forum* 7(4):237–41.

———. 1987. Freud revisited: On gender, moral development, and androgyny. *New Ideas in Psychology* 5(2):197–206.

———. 1987. Melanie Klein, psychoanalysis, and feminism. *Feminist Review* 25:23–37.

———. 1991. *Mothers of psychoanalysis: Helene Deutsch, Karen Horney, Anna Freud, Melanie Klein.* New York: Norton.

———. 1986. *Sexual contradictions: Psychology, psychoanalysis, and feminism.* London: Tavistock.

Schafer, Roy. 1976. *A new language for psychoanalysis.* New Haven: Yale University Press.

Schott, Robin May. 1988. *Cognition and eros: A critique of the Kantian paradigm.* Boston: Beacon.

Segal, Hanna. 1974. *Introduction to the work of Melanie Klein.* New York: Basic Books.

———. 1983. Some clinical implications of Melanie Klein's work. *International Journal of Psycho-Analysis* 64(3):269–76.

Sennett, Richard. 1981. *Authority.* New York: Vintage.

Showalter, Elaine. 1987. *The female malady: Women, madness, and English culture, 1830–1980.* New York: Penguin.

Silverman, Doris K. 1987. Female bonding: Some supportive findings for Melanie Klein's views. *Psychoanalytic Review* 74(2):201–15.

Simpson, Evan. 1987. Moral conservatism. *The Review of Politics* 49(1):29–58.

Spelman, Elizabeth V. 1988. *Inessential woman: Problems of exclusion in feminist thought.* Boston: Beacon.

Spillius, Elizabeth Bott. 1983. Some developments from the work of Melanie Klein. *International Journal of Psycho-Analysis* 64(3):321–32.

Stack, Carol B. 1986. The culture of gender: Women and men of color. In Linda K. Kerber et al., On *In a different voice:* An interdisciplinary forum. *Signs* 11(2):321–24.

Sullivan, Edmund V. 1977. A study of Kohlberg's structural theory of moral development: A critique of liberal social science ideology. *Human Development* 20(6):352–76.

Taylor, Charles. 1977. What is human agency? In *The self: Psychological and philosophical issues,* edited by Theodore Mischel, 103–35. Oxford: Oxford University Press.

Tronto, Joan C. 1987. Beyond gender difference to a theory of care. *Signs* 12(4):644–63.

———. 1989. Women and caring: What can feminists learn about morality from caring? In *Gender/body/knowledge: Feminist reconstructions of being and knowing,* edited by Alison M. Jaggar and Susan R. Bordo, 172–87. New Brunswick, N.J.: Rutgers University Press.

Unger, Roberto Mangabeira. 1984. *Passion: An essay on personality.* New York: Free Press.

Volkan, Vamik D. 1988. *The need to have enemies and allies: From clinical practice to international relations.* Northvale, N.J.: Jason Aronson.

Volkan, Vamik D., Demetrios A. Julius, and Joseph V. Montville, eds. 1990. *The psychodynamics of international relationships.* Vol. 1, *Concepts and Theories.* Lexington, Mass.: Lexington Books.

Wallach, John R. 1987. Liberals, communitarians, and the tasks of political theory. *Political Theory* 15(4):581–611.

Walzer, Michael. 1990. The communitarian critique of liberalism. *Political Theory* 18(1):6–23.

Williams, Bernard. 1973. *Problems of the self: Philosophical papers, 1956–1972.* Cambridge: Cambridge University Press.

Westkott, Marcia. 1989. Female rationality and the idealized self. *The American Journal of Psychoanalysis* 49(3):239–50.

Winnicott, Donald Woods. 1987. *Babies and their mothers.* Reading, Mass.: Addison-Wesley.

———. 1958. *Collected papers: Through paediatrics to psycho-analysis.* New York: Basic Books.

———. 1965. *The maturational processes and the facilitating environment.* New York: International Universities Press.

———. 1971. *Playing and reality.* London: Tavistock.

Young, Iris Marion. 1987. Impartiality and the civic public: Some implications of feminist critiques of moral and political theory. In *Feminism as critique: On the politics of gender,* edited by Seyla Benhabib and Drucilla Cornell, 56–76. Minneapolis: University of Minnesota Press.

———. 1983. Is male gender identity the cause of male domination? In *Mothering: essays in feminist theory,* edited by Joyce Trebilcot, 129–46. Savage, Md.: Rowman and Littlefield.

Index